Confessions from a **HELL BOUND TAXI**

Book 2: ***Wicked Women of Misery City***

OFFICIAL FIRST EDITION

Copyright 2016 ♠ Alaric von Boerner

✠✠✠✠✠✠✠✠✠✠✠✠✠✠✠✠✠✠✠✠✠✠✠

Confessions from a

HELL BOUND TAXI

BOOK 2

Wicked Women of Misery City

by
Alaric von Boerner

Published By
Ragnaroc Productions
P.O. Box 88
Stockton, California
95203

✠✠✠✠✠✠✠✠✠✠✠✠✠✠✠✠✠✠✠✠✠✠✠

"I would rather be exposed to the inconveniences attending too much liberty than to those attending too small a degree of it."
-- Thomas Jefferson

Back Cover: Page from original draft
written in Spencerian Script with a fountain pen

Introduction

I was driving taxi in San Francisco when my girlfriend went out of town and left her son with me. Then the boy had a brain hemorrhage, and I couldn't get a hold of his mother... Because it turned out she was with another boyfriend in Costa Rica.

Her boy was like my son, so I took care of him, and when I was signing the papers for emergency surgery at the hospital my dog got run over by a car. I was having a bad day.

I hadn't checked my mailbox at work, so; while my dog was in surgery I went to check -- to find I had a termination notice. In 7 days I'd be out of a job. Within the week I got 4 tickets -- I hadn't got a ticket in 6 years, but suddenly my license would be revoked.

I drove all over looking for a job, and in the process got cited in various jurisdictions for expired tags -- I didn't know it was serious -- I was just broke, looking for a job. Then my car was vandalized, and not drivable – but now I had court appearances scattered around the State. Before reality kicked in I got a job driving cab in Hayward... Driving again, I got a call to a bar, and a Hells Angel that had chased everyone out of the bar needed a ride... Why me?

Then, my next fare didn't have the money, and I had to go into his apartment to collect... It took a long time to get paid... All in nickels! By the time I got outside the taxi had been towed away.

Fired for that, of course, I went home to make a new plan, but found out that my apartment had been raided by the FBI & ATF... My roommate had done something?

I drove East as if escaping the avalanche of problems. With no plan in mind I ended up in a strange place called Stockton.

Somehow, with 27 entries on my driving record I got a job driving a cab again. Then I got a house with nothing down, and moved in two fancy hookers to make the payments.

Was it luck, or had I died and went to Hell?

This is the incredible TRUE story of a Stockton City Cab driver.

Stockton, California
1992

Confessions from a Hell Bound Taxi
Book 2:

Wicked Women of Misery City

Driving taxi in Stockton had me immersed into a new life within a few of weeks, and in a very peculiar way. Like waking from a nightmare only to find the real world more frightening. No, I wasn't ruminating about how fate had landed me in this place. I was already tangled up in a new adventure – in a wild place that might be considered to be a laboratory to the world of what might happen to them.

On one dreary night I was driving up to 60 MPH down darkened streets alongside broken sidewalks ripped up by giant Oaks. The sidewalks seemed to be rising up like tombstones. There was no sign of life other than the dogs. Thick tulle fog swirled to open a peek-a-boo view of the packs of dogs disappearing between one house and the next.

Whatever anyone up in this town was doing, they were nowhere to be seen, and it was time for a dog to prowl in the still of the night. Spaniel would meet Beagle, and team up with a Shepherd. And there was plenty of what you get if you mix a lot of breeds, so it was ascertainable that this dog party had been going on for some time.

Dogs owned the streets by midnight. A few streets had people – compact mobs of people hiding between buildings, in doorways, or in certain areas where the fog was especially thick – all engaged in some sort of dirty deeds.

I raced toward downtown Stockton in hopes of hunting down some human life -- perhaps a customer willing to pay. Suddenly a girl jumped out of nowhere. I whipped around the block to take another look, but she was gone. She had vanished as if swallowed up by the fog, and I wondered where she could've gone, but the weirdness of it all didn't leave me wondering long. I quickly resumed racing down the road.

An impatient distaste rose up as if choking me as I approached the concrete cesspool known by the name of downtown Stockton -- In a town who's citizenry sometimes boasted of their highest crime per capita status. The community's claim to fame was a highly publicized mass murder of school children, reiterated in the media whenever the slightest opportunity arose. Oh, what evil lurks in downtown Stockton tonight?

My objective was as a hunter seeking prey -- a customer to convey for pay -- while avoiding becoming a victim myself.

As my desperate search continued I hoped to at least break even for the night. The streets looked back at me like a personal enemy, defying my survival.

Finally, I saw a figure moving in the shadows. Could it be a prospect? A citizen who for some unseemly reason had been vexed with being stranded downtown? Someone who didn't know when the bus stopped running; or had their car stolen? He may need a ride, or he could be in danger as I saw him walking toward a den of crime.

Taxi services are so needed by common criminals that I'd be much less at risk of being a victim than the man on the street, however, everyone out on these streets at night is at risk -- and this guy could be in danger if he didn't take a ride, or; he might be someone I'd better leave alone.

Anyone can become the next entry in the police blotter, and I couldn't rely upon the pecking order of preference to save me, so I carefully scrutinized all prospects like a predator might survey potential prey. Out of the corner of my eye I glanced at the man walking down the sidewalk. Acting totally disinterested I slyly weighed the situation. I saw some potential in what was perhaps a common drunk who might need a ride, and considered circling the block. Zipping around I quickly scanned for another possible catch -- perhaps a bigger fish.

Up ahead, shrouded by a foggy mist, I saw a gathering under a street lamp. For some reason the fog was not as thick downtown, and I could see 4 or 5 people on the corner. I made a quick turn onto California Street, and saw another half-dozen people up the block. From the looks of it, not one of these people could be considered a legitimate customer, just people best to be avoided.

More figures appeared, as if the living dead were emerging from the fog. On this particular block of California Street tonight, at this very moment, was a collage of rather gruesome social phenomena. The drunk, approaching from down the street would be certain to meet his doom. I put my foot to the floor and circled back to take another look.

I moved forward on a potential rescue mission, passing rows of darkened buildings that held a monument to a brighter past for Stockton... Right down the street is the oldest bank in California, where more than a century ago, weary miners may have made their way to a booming metropolis here in the middle of the Big Valley.

Like many towns from the Gold Rush days, it looked like Stockton wanted to become a ghost town too, and would have, were it not for its location in the center of the richest agricultural region in the world.

After farming, drug smuggling and whores made up the businesses that were doing it big, and these days, not a weary miner, but a different element came downtown, especially at night, looking for a different kind of gold.

At night a massive drug bazaar opened throughout the streets, and prostitutes strut about everywhere. At 5:30 p.m. the Border Patrol shut down, and the show began -- swarms of wetbacks appeared; as well as hookers, dope dealers, and a fabulous mix of sleaze that all converged upon Downtown. Death also walked the streets at night in Stockton.

As I came around the corner I saw the drunk again, staggering in the shadows in what I truly believed was the wrong direction for him to be going safely. He was wearing a dark green sport coat and khakis. He was a large man that had a build suggesting a construction worker, but overall he really looked like a clerk – growing larger and less fit. I made sure he saw me, but he looked at me like I'm stupid -- then he walked over to the other side of the street. Perhaps it would be a good idea to circle the block again and pull up in front of him even if I had to offer him a free ride a few blocks so he might avoid the dire straits directly in his path. Just then, Mean Marion bellowed over the radio; "79, get Harvey's bar." Radio orders are a priority, and Harvey's was only two blocks away, so I abandon my reluctant prospect.

I arrived at Harvey's in less than a New York minute and

ran into the bar hollering; "Taxi". Almost everyone in the bar knew me by now after running in hollering almost every night over the past month, but nobody wanted a cab.

The bartender gave me a dollar just for showing up.

As I was leaving, a girl came out from a corner in the bar, and tried to 'borrow' the dollar from me-- she followed me out of the bar.

Just outside, as I was explaining how borrowing the dollar was out of the question, another girl walked up on me jostling into position for my attention, and chased away the girl who was after my dollar.

This new confrontation looked as if she had a fashion designer from Ringling Brothers. A young white girl -- she starting talking with a heavy ghetto drawl:

"Me and my husband needs a cab."

"Where's your husband?" I asked.

"Around the corner."

"Where'd you want to go?"

"Look, we needs a cab!" she demanded.

"You got money?" I demanded.

Just then a black man appeared, evidently the 'husband' of this girl who dresses like a clown. Adding everything together seemed to spell industrial-strength trouble. Even so, as I was about to get into the cab, I looked her straight in the eye and asked again; "Where do you want to go?"

"We'll tell you," she said.

But I had enough of her suspicious behavior, and didn't like the looks of her 'husband' either.

"No," I said, "I've got to pick someone else up in a minute, so if I'm going to take you anywhere, I'm going to have to know where it is you want to go."

"What?! You don't want to take us?" she said, continuing her confrontational demeanor.

"I didn't say that." I replied, in a calm, but firm tone.

"You're racist!" the girl shouted. Just then, the black man started tugged wildly at my appropriately locked door.

The accusation, *Racist*, can be very emotionally charged, and detract from what's more important– like behavior, individual character, achievement, etc.

When race is emphasized we forget that the focus should be on the individual ...not the team we supposedly belong to. I like to look at people as Individuals, and these people were clearly some individuals that I didn't want anything to do with. Calling me a racist certainly wouldn't get them anywhere. The popular propensity for the argument should end, and the race card be torn up and thrown away forever.

As these weasels tried to find a way into the cab, I fondly remembered the other day...

While parked at the Greyhound station, a very arrogant and aggressive young black guy had jumped in my cab and started laying a lot of crap on me. Confusing conflict is often a tool used by people who want to take advantage— like rob you, maybe. It's not a good idea to give way to it, so, I yelled at him; "What are you trying to do, ruin my day?"

"See this?" he had said, as he proceeded to graphically exhibit the up-and-down motion of the door lock.

What a great guy he was to teach me that -- I never realized how wonderful a door lock could be, but tonight I was sure glad I had learned that lesson as I stood outside the taxi watching this crazy black man tug at the locked door.

As if it was just casual conversation, I calmly informed

this odd couple;

"You're trying to intimidate me, you're arguing, you're yelling, and people out at night are up to no good, so I'm leaving."

With the man still savagely tugging at the door, and the girl knocking hard on the window, I jumped into the cab and burned rubber. The dramatic departure emphasized my point, and also brought the attention of the dope dealers on the street—the bosses of the streets—who didn't like cab drivers being messed with.

The taxi provided important support services for the drug trade. And *general principals*, or any excuse could provoke a thrashing by the drug dealers in charge -- notably if the transportation system was threatened.

The couple quickly forgot about trying to catch a cab and slipped away.

Exactly on the next corner happened to be the drunken wanderer, and this time he flagged me down. He decided he wanted a cab after all. He was standing amongst five other people on the corner as I pulled up. I unlocked the door, and one of the people in the crowd opened it, poked his head in, and said in a 'dope deal friendly' tone;

"What's you need?"

"Nothing," I said; "The guy behind you needs a cab."

"Oooooh," he said, nodding his head up-and-down slowly.

As he proceeded with a feeble attempt at unrelated small talk, I wondered; does he think I pulled up for the purpose of inane conversation, or what?

Then I snarled at him; "Get out of the door."

He stepped back with a fancy shuffle. The drunk

proceeded to get into the cab. I continued to give the would-be conversationalist the 'crazy eye'.

Just as the drunk sat down in the back seat there was a big fuss in the small-group standing outside of the cab. Then one of them said; "Hey that's my cab!" Then another in the crowd came forward to offer assistance.

"Here, let me give you hand," he said, as he firmly grabbed my customers arm to usher him out.

While all of this was going on someone came around to my window to distract me, and before I knew it the drunk was out, and two fools were in the back seat talking to each other:

"Hey, where you want to go?" said one.

"I don't know," said the other. Then he asked me; "You accept food stamps?"

I snapped at them; "Get the hell out, and close the door!"

They got out without another word and closed the door.

I opened the front door to let the drunk back in. As he approached, staggering, one of the crowd pushed the door shut, and then blocked the customers advance toward it.

"Open the door," I yelled.

At this, a pair in the group began skipping around in circles, and a silly manner, chanting; "Open the door. Close the door. Open the door. Close the door." Then they started opening and closing the doors, which had all managed to become unlocked.

It became obvious at this point that this poor old drunk wasn't going to get a taxi. He wasn't just being mugged--he was being mobbed.

I drove away, and dialed the pay phone around the corner...

" 911, your emergency, please?" said the operator.
"This guy's getting robbed at California & Weber," I said.
Again, the operator; "911, what is your emergency?"
I hollered into the phone; "Hello, can you hear me?"
The voice came back from the phone again; "Hello."
Obviously the phone was out of order, but...

Within moments, a police car drove by, a rare sight when you need one. As the patrol car pulled up towards the phone I had used I notice that the whole crowd of people on the street had mysteriously disappeared.
At this point the drunk was in my cab. I brought him over to the officers who were now inspecting the phone.
"It doesn't work." I said to the officers.
The officers continued investigating the phone.
I yelled at them; "I called."
As if they didn't hear me -- an officer acted like he was going to inspect the phone some more while his partner was warily looking around. They paused for a moment, and then both of them turned to hear what I had to say, but didn't seem to be listening. Done with inspecting the phone, one of the officers took it upon himself to inspect my passenger's drunkenness. With robot like precision, the officers were at work.
Finally I got across to the officers that it was all about a robbery. Suddenly there was no more work to do. Evidently not, as one of the officers asked; "What are we supposed to do? They're gone now."
Irritated by the facts of the matter, especially after watching the victim try to walk a straight line, I decided to see if I could get away with taking command of the

situation; "Well, there's nothing left to do downtown, so we'd all better get going," I said. I grabbed the drunks arm in the midst of what looked like another phase of the drunk test, and shoved him into the cab--while explaining to the officers; "Don't worry about him. I'll take him home." The officers seemed to think that was OK, because they just left without saying anything.

"So, where do you live?" I asked, as the patrol car sped away from us.

"Way over on the Eastside, but I haven't got any money."

"Mother of God, I know that, but I'm not going to leave you in this rat hole."

"OK, 638 S. David," burping; "I appreciate this, I'll pay you later."

"Forget it! Just relax and be happy."

"I'm happy to get away from here. I get robbed, and then I thought they'd arrest me. I'm very glad to get away."

"Well, that's one of my functions... Getaway Car."

By the time I got to S. David the guy had passed out in the back of the cab. I had a lot of trouble getting him up and out. I'm not going to throw an old walrus over my shoulder and make it very far -- let alone up the steps. I wasn't throwing him over my shoulder at all. I tugged every which way as he slept like a baby, and finally got him out onto his front lawn. Dripping with sweat from the effort to move him, I convinced myself that where he rested looked like a very comfortable spot to leave him. He'd wake up in the morning, not knowing how he got there. He wouldn't remember a thing, and there will be no lesson learned. Next week he just might be downtown doing the same thing again.

I'd really had enough for one night, but unfortunately, I didn't have enough money to turn in the cab and pay the lease fee. Like a homing pigeon I headed back through downtown to land at the greyhound -- hoping to catch a flag on the way. It wasn't going to be easy. I was third up for a radio call, second in line at the 'gray dog', and nothing but trouble was roaming the streets. I just had to wait at the Greyhound station and be patient. I fell asleep at the cabstand, dreaming about chauffeuring a Rolls Royce.

Sometime later the dispatcher woke me, hollering...

"Yes, I'm here," I answered, as if calling to a rescuer.

"Well, it's about time you woke up," she said knowingly; "Get 341 South Filbert. Let me know when you get there"

'Oh boy,' I thought, 'the projects -- what a trip to wake up for.' I needed one more fare to go home, and wasn't looking forward to it. A driver was shot there last week. I certainly wouldn't ever be going there in a Rolls. Oh, they'd like the idea, too. Yeah sure, uh huh. I felt lucky when it turned out to be a 'no go'. The customer wasn't there, and I decided to call it quits and go home in the hole.

The Perez Story...

As a taxi driver you may meet some very pleasant people, or you may come across what's nothin' nice. After a few months of driving in Stockton I'd become quite familiar with a variety of characters around town. A frequent encounter was one Eduardo.

Eduardo Perez liked the local bars downtown, and the little Mexican café -- and a lot of older gals seemed to like him, too. He was a nice guy who was always elated. The first time he hired my cab there was no way I could understand his requested destination, and this led to a suggestion of hostility. The old man retorted; "I speak English, I don't speak Okie!"

I began to laugh, amused at how so many residents here refer to all light skinned people collectively as Okie's. My laughter broke the argumentative mode. I demanded to know his name, and talked to him briefly about his life...

"Long time in Stockton," he said. "Got many friends I know 30 years."

Just short of a fistfight I got added to his list of friends, and from then on he would regularly request me by name, insisting for the bartender to tell the taxi dispatcher to make sure they sent the right driver. Often it was just to say "Hi", and he'd give me a dollar and ask me to come back later. Sometimes he didn't take a ride of all, just gave me a dollar several times for returning. He was a pleasant break from the frequent undesirable passenger, and I was his connection to friendly service.

The dispatcher sent me to an order at the card room one day, telling me that I would be picking up a gentleman named Perez.

The moment I pulled up in front of the club someone jumped into the cab. I had anticipated Eduardo, and proceeded to rudely eject the oriental looking gentleman who had climbed in.

"Hey, I've got to get Perez," I said, "Get out!"

He gave me a sad look of frustration -- as I waved my hand to brush him away.

"I am Perez," he insisted, pointing to a name tag.

I looked at him questioningly.

"Yes, I'm Perez, I'm Perez." He went on to tell me that he was Hawaiian, and about Hawaii, and other things about himself. His tongue had been thoroughly loosened by the drink, and he was quick to want to tell all.

"Alright," I said, after listening to a short story of his life; "So where are we going?"

"Too dirty one Phipps."

"What?" I asked, and he repeated the same gibberish a few more times – his last shots of whiskey still kicking in.

"Oh, is it 231 5th?"

He nodded to my guess, and I started off in what he apparently considered to be the wrong direction -- maybe a block out of the way, technically.

"Hey, where you going?" he protested.

"231 5th, isn't that right?"

"Go down San Joaquin."

"I thought it would be easy to go this way, but I'll go however you want."

"I don't want to go all over."

"No problem, I'm giving you a discount anyway."

"Cabdrivers always trying this and that," he muttered.

"What! Are you complaining?" I asked aggressively.

"No, I'm not complaining, I just don't want to spend a fortune."

I laughed at him, and started fooling around with the equipment in the cab to divert his attention. I backhanded the meter, moved the visor, adjusted the radio dial (even though the radio wasn't on), and began swinging the microphone by the cord saying; "Have fun, enjoy yourself." But this silliness proved to be an ineffective diversion, and he pushed to continue an argumentative dialogue.

"You're overcharging me!"

"OK, watch, I'll make this light." I floored it for a second and the four barrels growled as the car surged forward to make it through a yellow light. "There," I said, "I made it through the light, I risked your life to save you a quarter."

His eyes opened wide, and he said; "The cops will put the light on you."

"Hey, it would have cost you a quarter to wait for that light."

"You'll get ticket," he snapped back.

"See, that too. Look at all the trouble I go through for you -- risk a ticket and everything. Aren't you happy?"

"I'm happy, but..."

I interrupted him in the spirit of argument, saying, "You accuse me of trying to cheat you. I risked your life to save you a quarter..."

"I don't care about a quarter," he said.

By remaining silent from that point on -- I won the argument.

Momentarily I dropped him off at his fifth street house, and evidently he had enjoyed the argument after all. He was complaining about money, but when it came time to pay, he gave me a substantial tip.

As he got out of the cab, I told him; "I'll think about you next time I have a pineapple." He staggered away laughing.

♠ *Life's no fun if you take things too seriously* ♠

It'd been 142 days since I started driving taxi in Stockton, and it seemed like I knew everybody in town. There were no tourists or business travelers as were typical in San Francisco. For the most part I got the same people all the time, often a peculiar type of people who never left the valley; as well as a mix of transients from Mexico. It seemed like a border town sometimes, although quite far from the Mexican border.

Driving cab at night in Stockton was still like a party on wheels, but not a millionaire's cocktail party like San Francisco -- it was more like operating a drug shuttle and getaway car. Sometimes I got caught by people I had conflict with before...

"Hey, aren't you the cab driver that gave me a hard time about a week ago."

"No, that wasn't me." And I realized that I had to be a little more tactful with people who got out of line, because there was a likelihood that I'd run into the same fools again.

Perhaps the 59th largest city in America, it was still like a small town. It was also like the *Wild West* of modern times -- with shootouts going on all over the streets at night on a regular basis. I didn't want to get caught in the middle, and it made sense to get to know people in order to know whom you might end up having to deal with, and what situations to avoid.

The girls staying at my house finally raised issues themselves. One of the girls that I had rescued from 'The City' had come up with a boyfriend, and, relatively speaking, was doing good. Claiming *clean and sober*, she was ready to move into her new boyfriends place.

The other whore had already got bored with the opportunity to straighten out, stole someone's gun and disappeared--owing me $20. I was losing my renters, but it was time for me to move out of the basement -- where I'd been staying since I got the house *on a shoestring*. I was making enough to handle it on my own now, and would be better off to say 'good riddance' to renters.

The house and the yard were both a mess. We had cleaned up the place not long ago when we moved in, but a very large pile of garbage had accumulated already. The house was in bad shape in the first place, and it was time to clean it again and start fixing things up. There was a lot to do to the old shack. I figured it would take months to get everything done, and I could really use some help.

José was an 18-year-old who lived down the street. I had seen him walk by my house several times, and on more than one occasion he had asked me if I needed any yard work done. So, the next time I saw him walk by I asked him if he wanted to help me haul a bunch of trash out of the house, take it to the dumps, and I'd give him 20 bucks. He was thrilled at the offer and ready to start right away. I told him to come by at noon. Jose came by the next day at noon, as instructed, and started working hard and fast.

The house got cleaned out better than I had anticipated in just one afternoon. In the course of the clean up I mentioned a few things that needed to be fixed. José quickly repaired a window frame before I even figured out how I was going to do it myself--and without my asking. He insisted that he could fix everything around my house and take care of the yard too. He would put in a fabulous garden, and take care of everything if I would just hire him for a couple hours a day.

"I don't have that kind of money," I said.

"20 bucks is cool – I'll even work for 4 hours."

Reluctantly, in response to his pressing, I said; "Just for a couple of days, maybe, because I really do need some help around here, but I can't afford to pay anyone. Just for a couple of days, OK?"

"I can do more right now," he said, eager to work.

"No, no, come over tomorrow again at noon. You can work for couple of hours then."

Jose came over the next day at noon and worked all afternoon -- even after

I told him to stop. He cleared an area in the rather large backyard and started turning over the dirt with a shovel. I couldn't believe how much work he'd done in one day, even still; it looked like he was trying to start a big project. I confronted him about it. He begged me to allow him to work more than a couple days. I didn't think I could afford it, but on the other hand, he did so much work I felt I couldn't afford to not take advantage.

♠ *When you take advantage of someone else ... you set the stage to be taken advantage of yourself* ♠

I agreed that José could come over and work for $20 a day, but wouldn't guarantee for how long-- I just couldn't afford it. Within a week Jose had fixed a door, repaired part of a roof, rebuilt a fence, and turned over the dirt in nearly half of the very large yard. He talked to me as if he was insisting that he wanted a permanent job. I didn't say anything. Maybe I can afford $100 a week, or maybe I could find some work for him to do for someone else—I thought about it. He was certainly a very good worker. I just wasn't in a position to be an employer.

Then Jose asked if he could rent my tool shed for $25 a month. There was still a lot of work to do, and I figured he wanted to put some tools in there.

He was so determined, and I certainly knew what it was like to be down and out. Maybe I could afford it for a little while, and José insisted he could work for $300 a month.

"OK, I'll rent you the shed, and you can show up at noon every day."

José worked furiously to build a garden, even when I wasn't there, and it was quite a project because it must have been about a quarter acre -- just weeds and garbage when he started. Jose asked for an extension cord that he could run out to the tool shed, and I didn't think anything of it. I happened to have a long extension cord that would reach, and I figured he wanted to use some power tools. He had repaired so many things around the place without any instruction or supervision.

The next day I noticed that José had fit in a love seat; had an end table to set a TV on, and had managed to get cable TV hooked up to the tool shed. I've had many encounters with things strange, but this was something new. I figured I'd better find out a little bit more about José's world. Was he living in my tool shed? What've I got into?

José's family lived down the street. He told me about his family, and I got the impression that most of the family didn't accept him very well because he had a different father. He had seven sisters and five brothers, all with the same mother. The oldest was 21, and three of the sisters had children of their own. Over 20 people in Jose's family were living in a two-bedroom house just down the street. José *really was* trying to live in my tool shed. I could see his point, but I couldn't see how I could agree with it.

Oh no, I had a guy living in my tool shed now. People said I should let him live in the house. He was in already. I had entrusted Jose with a key to the house so he could fix things, and he was in the house most of the time.

His family was entitled to come over to visit, of course, so... a mob of children converged on my house. I hadn't thought of that. Whatever José had fixed, might get torn.

"They're just visiting," said José. "They're just kids," said José. Then José got me figuring ... they had torn up that two-bedroom house that they were living in, blamed the landlord for not fixing things, and managed to delay an eviction process -- like they had done repeatedly on all sides of town. It was only a matter of time, and they'd all be living in a single motel room again. I couldn't wait, and hoped it would be far away. Jose asked me if I would please let them set up a teepee in my backyard, since it was such a large backyard, and his family could live there. I gasped, but then couldn't stop laughing.

I had to get rid of Jose, but I had the whole family to deal with now, too.

José had brought me over to have a beer with his mother, and they had all been over to my house; and once I knew them all I couldn't just un-know them so easy.

For a short time I was a treated as such a good friend of the family, and got to know them fairly well. Prudence should be wary. I noticed that they would steal from each other. I had a long conversation with one of the kids about his cousin stealing his bicycle from him. He acted as if it was normal, and it seemed that stealing was interpreted as a type of sharing. Soon, I would become a really bad guy to them -- because I didn't like sharing that way.

The kids were trying to steal bicycles in the neighborhood with the same tenacity as seen in José's work. Concerned about what was going on with this family, I went over to talk to their mother, and told her that she needed to teach the kids not to steal.

Her response was; "The kids gotta have stuff too."

Suddenly I was the enemy, but anyone outside of the family was normally the enemy anyway. There were social workers, and police, and other nosey people -- all of which, the kids were raised to hold with extreme suspicion. Any interference from outside posed a threat to a rather large welfare check. Mom drank at least a case of beer every day, and dad was a heroin addict—they needed the money.

I had offered advise to a few members of the family, and failed to realize that they didn't have a clue what I was talking about -- yet they pretended to understand quite well, just to get along and see what they could get. I was clearly an alien.

Running wild in the general population, they confined interaction within a familiar group, not communicating with people outside of their network except to rob them. If there was a ladder that could move them up, it was a flimsy one, and rose to a world that they could never relate to. The social network that could pull them up did not exist, and if anything, there might be pressure to knock them down.

Some of the kids had grown up never having a friend outside of their family, but there were plenty of cousins and other relatives -- an extended family of maybe 300 people. They had enmeshed themselves into their own private world. Herein was a good argument for partitioning people that can't get along on the same page. They certainly had a system for doing such themselves--with oddities too complex to describe.

One of the brothers went to his sister's work to take up some issue. As hard as it is to get a job, he thought nothing of disrupting her work and making her cry in the process. The brother did this simply because he didn't like his sister's boyfriend. That issue couldn't wait? I either needed to build a wall against these people, or find a place to hide. Who knows what they might do?

> ♠ *Social interaction, and engagement in any system, is powerful...*
> *... especially when we're confused about who we are as individuals* ♠

The way a dysfunctional family system works is something like this: Suppose dad is a drunk. Dad shouldn't be a drunk, but he is, and usually isn't at home. When he is at home, he beats up big brother -- so big brother is gone and out on the streets all of the time. Since dad and big brother aren't around, little brother gets to feel like he's the man of the house. Little sister takes care of big brother's puppy and it's becoming her own. Mom has too much to do, and big sister takes pride in helping out around the house. Then, dad quits drinking. Dad should quit drinking, but when he does; big brother comes around again and wants his puppy back from the little sister; little brother can't pretend he's man of the house anymore, and since dad is helping out, mom doesn't need big sister's help so much anymore. The family had learned to cope with a bad situation, but when dad quits drinking everyone else in the family shifts roles -- and they might not have even been aware of the roles that they were playing before. Suddenly they aren't coping anymore, and coping was a desperate issue before, so the family could be sent into turmoil in the course of the adjustment. Dad quit drinking, but with an abrupt change in the family system someone else might develop a problem in the shift.

I looked around town at other families that had their own peculiarities, and contemplated how family systems affected neighbors, and other people around them.

The neighborhood used to be an extension of family, but such neighborhoods didn't exist anymore.

Having a neighborhood pertinent to a particular lifestyle would allow for targeted social services, affordable housing, and other benefits... but who cares anymore.

A gap had developed between the family and the neighborhood. Dysfunctional families develop coping skills that enhanced their alienation, and this dysfunctionality generalizes to add up to a dysfunctional neighborhood.

The more wanting of substance and purpose people become, the more they find importance in roles, rituals, and labels. Gangs develop, holding up roles as a banner to meaningfulness even when they have no reasonable goals. To fill a void, rituals are enforced in order to emulate purpose. In the end, any game is better than no game, and with these people, unfortunately; the game often becomes cops and robbers. Violence, evictions, addictions, and going to prison are not viewed as things that disrupt one's life; they're just accepted as part of life – sometimes, as if without them there would be no life at all. I needed to insulate myself from Jose's world, or anything like it.

I used my real estate connections to find José somebody else he could work for -- but told him not to bring his family. Hopefully my problem would fade away, and I wouldn't be dumping it all on someone else.

Even with distancing myself from José, his family still considered that he was working for me, and complained to him; "Why do you have to work for that guy, why can't you get a job at McDonald's?" He was attacked for stepping outside of his vague and unspoken family-assigned role. I was the enemy, and still not at a comfortable distance. He wasn't going to a get a job at McDonald's, and he acted like his family wanted him to go live under the bridge anyway.

I hadn't noticed Jose downtown before, because he'd often been in jail. Now I recognized him every night downtown, smoking crack. If he wasn't lost in the world of the crack pipe, and he noticed me, he'd run over and ask me if I could find him some work; or if he could borrow a dollar. He had become a pest that wouldn't go away, but at least I managed to shake his family off my tail. The family just talked distastefully about me amongst themselves, which could appear threatening, but I knew better. They wouldn't be able to bother me if we weren't playing on the same game board.

My dog had puppies, but as soon as they were weaned, and the puppies bit her tit, she jumped over the fence, and got run over by a car. The last friendly contact I had with Jose's family was to give them an orphaned puppy.

♠ *Every game has a goal ...and even if we don't know that we're playing ... we're aimed at something.* ♠

At the beginning of my shift I'd leave the taxi lot and drive through downtown. It was rare for people to flag down a taxi without a lot of encouragement -- people in Stockton who wanted a cab would usually call on the phone. So, it made sense to head for the Greyhound bus station and sit on the taxi stand and at the same time wait for a radio call. I often pulled behind 4 other cabs that had the same idea. It was also a good idea to bring a book, because the wait could be long.

As I drove through downtown one day José tried to flag me down. I wasn't about to stop for him. It may be best to treat some people like they are poison. I had experience with other underprivileged people, and realized that my attempts to help them may have been because of my own sick personal vanity. The theory that social discord was because of the sad reality of *haves* and *have-nots* was a fraud. We want to believe that everyone is just like us, and wants the same things, but it isn't true – it's even selfish thinking. I'd offer a poor person $5, and instead of appreciate the gift they'd suddenly be asking for $20. If they couldn't get more gifts they knew I must have money to give away $5, and I may have inadvertently set myself up to be robbed. They'd say *poor people gotta steal*, as if it were the law of their universe. I'd try to explain that it works both ways: People who steal got to be poor, because a person will risk losing everything to steal something that might not have much value, and when stealing is an option they'll never suffer to learn how to earn things otherwise, so they stay stuck poor. People who steal hang around other people who steal, and they get along fine because none of them has anything. Trying to create opportunities for these people carries risk --

maybe I could just spare 5 bucks, but they'll just want more. I could be perceived as looking down on them, and hated for my help.

Trying to be a motivational speaker to the poor, and drag them up the ladder will likely fail. None will follow processes leading to opportunity. One guy who was hanging around me, frustrated because he really only wanted $5 or whatever, finally explained to me:

"We don't want to be rich, we just want to *feel* rich."

Rather than develop skills to get money, save it, invest it, etc.-- such a boring ambition is displaced by the thrill of sudden windfalls of thievery, and getting to waste the money, and feeling rich for a minute. The fool suffering to build real wealth had nothing on the guy with a gold chain sporting a giant dollar sign, or diamonds in a gold grill.

No, people don't think the same way. I was the one who was deprived in some people's minds – I had no bling. Actually, I hate jewelry. People don't like the same things.

Some people, like Jose--even if they are good people, could easily become trouble, simply because there is no way we are going to ever get on the same page.

I waved back at Jose --The best thing to do with some people is smile, and move on. I pulled up on the taxi stand, a little surprised that no other cabs were around.

The security guard's shift was about to change--perhaps the reason why no cabs were on the stand. The late night guard was something serious – claiming he took no prisoners, in a vicious way, and posing himself as a threat to everyone. He had the appearance of a gorilla, and came on his shift just to throw shit at anyone who looked at him.

I went inside the station to see if the coast was clear.

When I came back to sit in the cab I could see directly in front of the Greyhound station, about a half a block away, one of the other security guards (who was not so scary), escorting someone toward the station. I recognized who the guard was assisting. It was Gene, a blind man who likes to party, and recently used my taxi on several occasions. As I sipped a soda, watching the skinny security guard escorting Gene, it became evident that Gene wasn't enjoying the security guards assistance. As they came closer I got out of the cab to ask; "What seems to be the problem?"

"None of your business," the security guard answered in a cocky tone; "This guy was trying to walk on the freeway, and the police will have to take him somewhere."

The security guard for the Greyhound had taken it upon himself to leave his post, and go half a block away to bother someone-- and he said it was none of my business. Gene was struggling to break free as the guard called for police on his radio. Security made it unpleasant for some people, and this frail guard was doing his best to be an asshole. He found a blind man he could push around. I figured I'd stay...

The police arrived fairly quickly, and the guard said to them; "You're going to have to take this guy somewhere."

I immediately interrupted; "Oh, Gene, you need a ride?"

"You know him?" asked the officer.

"Sure, he walks around on his own all of the time, and I can't understand why the guard forced him over here from down the block."

The guard being began whining; "He was trying to go on the freeway!"

Again I interrupted; "I'll give him a ride, I know where

he lives," and by the rule of assumption – I began assisting Gene into the cab.

The police then turned to the guard, who was throwing a fit, and asked; "Haven't you got something better to do?"

We drove off, Gene complaining angrily; "A person can't even hitchhike anymore."

At about this time the girls were coming out. The streets of Stockton at night had a girl on every single corner -- 'Ladies of the Evening' they liked to be called. There were so many, it seemed to cause a price war -- because five dollars or even three dollars might get you something.

Gene didn't get such a bargain with them– he was an easy victim, being blind.

Recently he got a taxi ride straight to big trouble from some other driver. I'd watch out for Gene, as you'd hope people would do for a blind man. Some people would -- his favorite bar started keeping a bank for him so he wouldn't get taken to the cleaners again.

"Yeah, Gene, I'm sure glad you don't want a naughty girl for a change, they rip you off too much."

"No, just want to get a room right now." ...And Gene continued mumbling something about hitchhiking.

"This place is just trouble for you, Gene, I'm from the Bay Area, you'd probably do better there."

"No... I've been in the Bay Area, to Hell with that place too. I was in the Bay Area alright -- I was in San Quentin."

"San Quentin prison?"

"Yeah, I was the only person to ever escape from there."

"Are they still looking for you?"

"No, this was years ago. Then I went into the air-conditioning business in the 50's, and had my own business until I went blind."

As we neared a motel to try for a room -- with the night closing in; a girl on the corner let out a yell. It was Leslie. Leslie seemed like a nice girl, and probably not a thief. She didn't need to steal—not the way she worked. She was, however, quite definitely, absolutely crazy.

"Harry, George, hey Fred!" She yelled out names at random as people drove by her corner. She was wearing a long imitation leather coat, her long blond hair fluttered as she gyrated her body, and then... she opened her coat. She was completely naked underneath the overcoat.

I was glad Gene couldn't see, as we proceeded without interruption, and into the driveway of the Vagabond Inn.

As I ushered Gene into the lobby, we could still hear Leslie hollering in the distance; "Bob!... Larry!..." No doubt flashing some of the motorists as they drove by.

In the motel, the lady at the desk appeared slightly annoyed when I asked; "Do you have a room for this gentleman?" By the look on her I wondered if she knew Gene already—in a negative light.

"I don't think we have a handicapped room available."

"Does it have to be a special room?" I asked; "I can help him to his room."

"Let me check." She said, fumbling through some cards.

I asked Gene to sit down.

The lady continued fumbling.

I tried to steer Gene toward a chair.

The lady looked unhappy—still fumbling through cards.

Again I asked Gene to sit down. Then he reeled; "Don't tell me what to do!" Then he hit me square on the collar with his blind stick.

The lady stopped fumbling; "No way! He's too violent."

Personally, an armed and dangerous blind man wouldn't scare me too much, but we already knew that the desk clerk thought he might be too much of a problem -- and now she had a valid excuse not to rent. Just as well, we could find another place if Gene would cooperate.

He started swearing at the desk clerk at the next motel down the block—so that didn't work, either. As I helped him back into the cab again, I said;

"Look, I'm trying to help you out, and I don't want you to spend all of your money riding around in the cab. We have to find you a room."

"OK," he said, and appeared remorseful.

"Now where do you want to go?"

"I don't care."

"Do you want to go to the bar? I'll be happy to drop you off at the bar with friends -- rather than get beat with a stick, or some other trouble."

"No, try another motel," he said.

"Yeah, you've been drinking enough today. I've heard of you batting people with your stick in the Avenue Bar, too, but I didn't believe it. You're going to have to behave yourself if you want people to enjoy helping you out."

"Alright, alright, let's go."

"How about we try Motel 6?"

"Let's go."

We pulled up at the Motel 6, and I told Gene not to say a word; "Stay here," I told Gene, as I got out of the cab. I didn't want him to blow it, and needed to slip him into a room to get rid of him. I went to get the motel manager.

"I've got a poor old crippled blind man in my taxi, and does he have to come to sign in, or is there any way I can do it for him, or maybe you could come out to the cab and take care of things; then I'll drive him to the room and help him in— What do you say? I wasn't asking for yes or no; it was either/or. For the sake of business sense, and customer service, the desk clerk had to agree.

"Certainly, give me a minute and I'll be out with the receipt book and key."

I ran back to the cab. "Gene, be cool. Get out your ID, and the money, and just sign for the room. Don't even say anything, OK?"

The desk clerk came out and everything went smoothly.

After I got Gene to his room, it looked like he only had $15 left, and the meter was up to $22.

He'd need five dollars later to take a cab to the bank, so I told him; "Hey, just give me 10 bucks and we'll call it even."

I figured I'd make up for it with him later, since he'd been a regular customer that usually tipped well.

I wondered about Gene's wish to hitchhike – nobody did that anymore, but Gene didn't know – he'd been blind for a while. What would people think about him on the side of the road with his thumb out? He said he'd been the only prisoner to ever escape from San Quentin. Maybe he finally managed to hitch a ride, and escape from Stockton, because I never saw Gene again.

After dropping Gene off that night, I returned to the Greyhound bus station, and noticed a girl hanging around the taxi stand -- still no cabs around. I pulled up, and the girl got in the front seat -- often a signal of a problem customer.

In Stockton most people insisted upon riding in the front, and often were true to the cue -- trouble. This girl had a problem ...now I owned it, because she was in my front seat.

"Please," she said, "Help me out, I only need seven dollars to get back to San Jose. My friend stranded me here, and I don't know anything about this place, and it doesn't look too safe. I'm a little nervous -- nothing like this has ever happened to me before. Can you help me? I just need seven dollars more." She rambled on with a barrage of pleading until I interrupted her.

"You say your friend left you stranded?" I asked.

"Yeah, and I don't know how I'm going to get home -- I just need seven dollars."

"You say you don't know this place, but you know enough to think it's not safe. You sure you're not part of the problem? Didn't I see you around here a few months ago trying to get seven dollars for your babies milk?"

"No, I don't have a baby."

"I believe that," I acknowledged.

"I live in San Jose, and I need to get home. I never been here before, and I'm scared."

"Well, you're not scared to ask for seven dollars."

"Then you'll give it to me?"

"No, I didn't say that."

"Please, Mr. taxi driver, I know you're a good person, just seven little dollars."

"I don't even think I have seven dollars."

"Well, do you have six?"

"Interesting," I said laughing; "You ever sell used cars?"

"No, I just need to get to San Jose, please."

"What kind of work do you do?"

"I'm a waitress at Denny's in San Jose, and I'll lose my job if I don't get back there. Do you have just five or six dollars you can spare, please, please, please?"

"You live in San Jose?"

She replied with a puppy dog whine; "Yes, and I don't know this place-- it doesn't look safe."

"They have a security guard, you can hang around him -- there he is right there," I said.

The mean guard had come on duty, and was walking around the building. The girl saw him and ducked, saying; "No, I don't like that security guard, he's an ass hole."

"Why did you duck down?" I asked.

"I dropped something on the floor."

This wasn't the skinny guard I miffed before—this was monster trouble. I didn't dare ask for his help.

How did she know he was an asshole?

"I don't think you live in San Jose, I think you're the same girl with the sick baby."

"What baby?"

"Right... what baby?"

"No, really, I live in San Jose."

"OK, what city is next to San Jose?"

"Santa Clara."

"That's a lucky guess--name another city by there."

"I don't know that much, I haven't lived there very long."

"Yeah, right, and you're wasting your time here because I got no dough, lady."

"Oh, please just five dollars, please."

"Hey, I said I got no money, so why are you still here?"

"Aw, come on, you picked up some customers, you've got to have at least five dollars."

"No, sorry, I don't, whatever I got I owe, so you just have to get out and try somewhere else. Try milk for the sick baby, maybe that will work better this time."

"Five dollars?"

"No, go away."

"Look, I've never done anything like this before, but if you'll just give me three dollars, I'll… I'll …have sex with you." She blurted out deperately.

"No, afraid not," I said with a smirk.

The woman was rather large, not fat but husky, and talk wasn't working for her, so; she made a rather dramatic expression of desperate need on her face, and then acted as if she was going to lunge at me. It was an interesting gesture -- a skillful blend of intimidation and begging. This woman, who said her name was Roxanne, wasn't about to get out of the cab. She was holding me hostage for five dollars, or whatever.

I was having trouble figuring out how to get rid of her. Telling her to "get out" wasn't working, and then she said;

"If you don't give me $5 I'll say you tried to rape me."

"Nice try," I said, "I'm sure they'll believe that a husky woman like you could be raped without either one of us suffering a scratch. And as if I'm the only one in the world left for you to bother, can you go bother someone else?"

She persisted for over 45 minutes. I was growing ever more frustrated that she wouldn't just leave.

"You're robbing me of my time, and you'd make more at a minimum-wage job rather than badger me."

"I have a job," she said, "I just need to get to San Jose."

I knew better than to call the police—a waste of time, or I could get arrested on an erroneous claim. The conundrum continued...

Finally, I saw someone who might help -- a woman crossing the gas station next to the Greyhound. She looked like a hooker, and she also looked like she wanted a cab. Walking straight toward the cab, she ducked her head and stared straight at me trying to see who was in the cab. Certainly she wanted a cab, I thought, and she could help me get this other woman out so she could have one. Perhaps another street girl could help.

I jumped out to greet the woman as she approached; "Hey, you need a taxi?"

"Yeah," she said, "Who's that?"...as she pointed at my unwanted passenger.

"Oh, that bitch won't get out of my cab, maybe you can help me."

"Oh sure," she said, as if it would be no problem, and climbed into the back of the cab to tell Roxanne; "Hey, I've got to go somewhere, can you give this cab driver a break and get out so we can go?"

Roxanne smiled back at her; "He's going to give me five dollars first."

"No I'm not! I haven't got it for you."

The frail blond newcomer joined in; "Come on, miha, give the taxi driver a break, he hasn't got it."

This went on for a few minutes, and it was obvious we weren't getting anywhere, but at least I had a witness.

"Roxanne, look, you're interfering with my business -- if you don't get out you're going to jail."

"Go ahead, call the police, I'll tell them you robbed me," she replied.

I shifted to drive and flew out of the driveway into the

police station parking lot right across the street. I slammed on the brakes in hopes of drawing some attention, but there was no one around. I got out to see if I could find an officer to help me eject the bitch. As I stepped out of the cab Roxanne reached over the seat, snatch my pack of cigarettes, and took off running.

"Well, she got what she wanted," said the other girl, who was still sitting in the back; "Can you take me home now?"

I was enraged, but relieved to be rid of the problem, and didn't want to take it out on this other girl ...she seemed kind of nice.

"Where do you live?" I asked, as I pulled out of the driveway.

"Over by Hwy 99, in a mobile home park."

We made it a couple blocks when the girl revealed that she didn't have any money. I pulled to the curb; "What? Who's going to pay for the cab?"

"Well, I thought since I helped you get rid of that girl."

"Come on! ...Did you help?"

"I've had a bad night," she said, "And you're making it worse."

"Get out," I told her; "That'll make my night better."

"No," she said.

Oh, shit—'never give a sucker an even break', and I was it. I felt insanity creeping up on me. "To hell with it," I said, and proceeded to drive like a maniac across town to dump this trash in the trailer park.

Along the way the dispatcher called; "79, you have a personal." I answered curtly, "I'm busy," turning my attention back to my problem customer.

With the nuisance finally ejected, I called back to the

dispatch; "79 is vacant, where is the personal?"

The dispatcher didn't give an address, and simply said; "Its Mary," mocking my manner when I told her "I'm busy," but that's all I needed to know. Mary had called for me personally quite regularly over the past week, and tied me up for quite a spell a couple of times. Relying on her claim of being an heiress, I did manage to persuade her out of $80 in order to spend most of the evening with her once -- an incident of which she has constantly reminded me, claiming, it seems, that I would forever owe her. At this point Mary was becoming a real gamble. Would she really want to pay for a ride? Sometimes she just wanted me to hang around. Or there would be a weird emergency that I, supposedly, was the only person who could be of help. One point for putting up with all of this was that Mary was quite beautiful -- a petite 23-year-old whose true claim to fame was that she was once on the Olympic gymnastics team.

Off to see Mary I went, telling myself that this time I would be firm. I won't allow her to waste any of my time.

I rang the bell and Mary appeared, opening the door wide and smiling. My strength of being firm crumbled as she gyrated in front of me in a skimpy lace nightgown.

"Can you come in?" she said, in a sexy voice.

Her gown had little heart-shaped holes with embroidered red borders. I stood there stunned, as if counting the little red hearts that draped her exquisite body. Impatient with my fascination, she snapped: "Come in!" She opened the door wide. I floated in the door as if riding on a wave of the delicious vanilla-like scent of her perfume. Inside her apartment I shifted back into reality as she said; "Sit down while I change. We have to go somewhere."

Mary changed her clothes rather quickly—I was surprised. She came back into the room within just a few minutes. She was wearing tight denim jeans and a ruffled white blouse with little pink elephants all over it. She looked at me and smiled, arched her back slightly as if standing tall for her 5' 4" stature, and stood erect as if she was going to spring into the air, an angel in flight. Diamonds seemed to rise from her smile. Her breasts stood at attention. I was willing to waste some time, I thought.

"I want to go to Mariani's and back, are you ready?"

"Yeah," I said, trying to steady myself.

"Well, let's go," she said, "I'll get the baby."

I shuddered, disgusted at the thought of the baby -- knowing that Mary's intention was to go to a very dangerous spot, and buy drugs.

Mary was absolutely thrilled about her baby, constantly fussing about her precious little princess, and so concerned that a microorganism from another person might get near it -- but she didn't mind bringing it on a dope run. She'd laud over her baby's beauty with me nodding in agreement.

"Isn't she cute?" Mary said, as she held up her baby.

It was the ugliest baby I'd ever seen—damned butt ugly. Something was clearly wrong-- the results of some sort of toxic indulgence for sure.

Mary brought out a car seat to put in the cab, and carefully strapped in her crack baby, while incessantly asking me; "Isn't she beautiful?"

Such a shame we have to lie to women, but in this case honesty would have been a greater evil. I just didn't say anything, and then reasoned that I should say something; "Do you really think we should take the baby to Mariani's?"

Mary responded indignantly, as if I'd expressed my true opinion on baby's beauty; "Hey, I don't want to discuss it!"

There was no baby sitter, and the precious troll wasn't to stay home alone, so the three of us were all off on Mary's drug mission. Mary handed me five dollars in advance.

Mariani's was the Grand Central Station for drugs, conveniently located right across the street from the police station parking lot.

Most of the traffic involved cocaine, in contrast with California Street where heroin dominated the menu, but either place could have anything—even people who had nothing to do with drugs.

Actually, Mariani's was a respectable working mans clothing store on the corner, but people who asked to go to Mariani's usually weren't going to buy clothes.

We pulled up on El Dorado Street, a long block right in between the clothing store and the police station back lot. There was a large crowd there, all of very questionable character—a more beaten down crowd than over on California Street.

The place was very dangerous, and the close proximity to the police station provided no relief.

"Mary," I said, "I don't want any of these people near my cab... and the baby of course."

Oblivious to my concern, she said; "Stop right here."

"Maybe you should call it off and go home. I won't charge you for the ride. You shouldn't have the baby here."

She ignored me -- starring down the block. She patted her coat pocket as she stepped out into the cluttered street. "I've got my gun," she said.

As she exited the cab, anxious fiends and dealers surrounded her. The dealers haggled against each another for her business, and the fiends tried to mediate for a percentage, or just beg for a crumb.

I can give people rides, but I make sure I have nothing to do with their business. As I sat waiting for Mary, I observed how much I wanted nothing to do with it. I watched disdainfully.

A woman was creeping down the street, bent over and picking up things and putting them in her mouth. She worked her way down the gutter not once standing up straight -- tasting every piece of white garbage along the way in her craving for a taste of more cocaine.

The woman was totally immersed, stuck on a truly idiotic mission. The crowd around her ignored the woman -- many appeared to be equally stuck on stupid, pursuing a variety of ridiculous nonsense. There was not one smile in this crowd. There was no laughing Even the few creepy personages who were puffing pipes in doorways appeared to get no satisfaction. The part of their brain that knows or feels anything was turned off—and perhaps, slowly melting away.

My attention was drawn away from the hoard of crack monsters, to notice a sort of shopping cart wagon train coming around the corner -- A young black man struggling at the helm. In the world of people who would hold all of their worldly possessions in shopping carts, this was perhaps a man of great wealth.

In creating such a spectacle as he did, struggling with a half a dozen shopping carts strung together, he got enough attention to imitate fame.

He surely looked proud as he tugged at his train of trash.

Truly, the only even remotely happy soul on the block-- he had the same blessings as the rich and famous, without the burden of responsibility.

Who could wish for more?

The scene on the block certainly left a lot to be hoped for, but at this moment I just wished Mary would hurry. I wondered how anyone could do this, how anyone could be in this... but I was there, and liking it less every minute.

Some fool near my cab, poisoned with crack, was twisting about like a contortionist, and this sent the baby into a squealing frenzy. The baby also needed its diapers changed.

Suddenly I realized that Mary had disappeared, but it was almost as if I didn't care.

The meter ticking away to questionable prospects, the baby's awful screen, the fool on drugs doing an involuntary dance, and the rancid stench rising from the streets– it all overloaded my capacity to relate, and left me numb as I watched the train of shopping carts disappear into the haze of the night.

I just sat there stunned, blending into those around me who were stunned by their drugs. I suddenly realized ... the tramp tugging the carts of trash, the dealers, and the dope fiends on the street... the claims of success and greatness by Mary, and her fuss about her baby-- all of these things were holding up the same message: The need for people to feel important, to be recognized, to have a game, a mission, a purpose in life. It doesn't matter what the imagined purpose in life is-- they are all illusions. I wondered if careful observation would make it possible to reveal that not only these people, but even the regular good citizen might have cheated themselves; believing what they believe, and submitting to the slavery of one routine or another-- for the sake of some shortsighted fancy.

People are encouraged to think too much about what they can get, and lose focus on the value of what they do -- dope fiend or not. I sat there as if watching the world go to Hell -- riding a train of processes over purposefulness.

Finally, Mary emerged from a crowd surrounding a doorway down the block. She ran back to the cab and hopped in. I pulled away from the curb with a screech of the tires and careened wildly in my departure -- To suggest a maniac taxi would encourage people to stay out of my way.

With the dope in hand, Mary didn't mind one bit that I drove her and her baby so recklessly back to her house. To her pleasure, despite the potential hazards, we made it to the location of the necessary crack pipe in seconds. It had been just a moment since she puffed a borrowed crack pipe, and she was already in a hurry for more. Crack cocaine doesn't really give you much of a high, and it only lasts a few seconds. The most important part of the high, perhaps, is the feeling that you're doing something important. As we pulled up to the house Mary became frantic.

"Hurry up," she said; "Take my keys and open the door while I get the baby." "Come on sweetums," she said, as she carried her baby to the door.

Once inside, she decided that I was going to smoke crack with her. I pulled a 'Bill Clinton', but she detected something wrong.

"Here, let me show you how to do it," she said, as she held the pipe to my face.

"No," I protested, "I don't like to do it that way."

"Well! We shouldn't be in here with my precious baby anyway -- come into the bathroom." She grabbed my hand, and led me into the latrine. The bathroom suggested a little naughtiness, and I anticipated some excitement in close quarters with Mary on drugs.

I began to run my hand up her thigh. I put my hand up her back, under her blouse; her body was such a thrill, so soft, yet firm.

Suddenly she became gruff, "We can't leave the baby out there alone," she said, and abruptly left me sitting there alone on the toilet.

Before I had a chance to feel stupid I was saved by the bell – someone was at the door, ringing. Mary ran over to me...

"It's the cops," she whispered.

"No, the cops didn't follow us. There was no reason to be singled out like that." I pointlessly suggested that she was just paranoid. I looked out the peephole on the door, and on the other side, under the yellow bug light, stood another one of the cab drivers. I opened the door.

"Hey, what's up?" I asked.

"Hey, it's busy, we need you out here. The dispatcher keeps whining," said the driver, who had come out of curiosity more than duty.

I left Mary to deal with her paranoid crack craziness on her own, and went out to get back into the cab.

I pressed the microphone button; "79."

The dispatcher crackled back over the radio; "79, where have you been? We've been busy. Get the Aurora Club."

She might have been busy for a minute, but it was a slow night, and she was just irritated about me disappearing sometimes. I left Mary's apartment without saying goodbye, and headed off to the order.

The Aurora Club was a bar where the customers often didn't speak English, and often weren't even there by the time the taxi arrived -- which was the case this time.

I called in to the dispatcher; "79 has no go."

"All right 79, you're 5th cab Central."

It was a slow night with no luck.

I finished the shift without enough to buy a pack of cigarettes.

On the next day, an uneventful day, I only took home $15, but had plenty of time during my shift to read a book called 'The Ring Cycle'. At least a good book made it a welcomed change from the nightmare of the previous night.

The last few days of the month were pretty rough. Often drivers would go in the hole to the company. But, if you didn't work the end of the month you might not get to work the first -- which was crucial, because taxi drivers in Stockton made half of their income in the first five days of the month, so...

Another painfully slow day was to come, the taxi stands at Amtrak and the bus station were both full of cabs, and I didn't want to hang around the normal spots just to read another book. I amused myself by fantasizing that I was Siegfried from the Ring Cycle, and passed the time driving around imagining I was on a quest for the mythical warrior woman, Brunhilde. I saw a few warrior women, but not of a breed that would suit my fantasy.

Still early into my shift, I parked at Mariani's, where the robust drug trade held out even when the rest of the town was quiet. I sat at this rather dangerous spot for nearly an hour to risk the chance of a fare.

Suddenly a wild woman came barreling down the street hollering something. As she approached the cab she called at me as if she knew me -- but I didn't remember ever seeing her before. And no, this certainly wasn't Brunhilde.

"Hey, you want some good pussy?" she said, as she jumped into the cab.

She continued, talking as if she knew me well; "Hey, these people don't know what's up. You know how to do it! You got the big dick, and I've got the good pussy. These people are nowhere. Let's get out of here and I'll suck your dick." She continued rambling on about sex as I drove off.

"Hurry up, let's get the hell out of here," she said.

I didn't care to be her getaway car, and drove off rather slowly.

I'd never met such an extremely aggressive woman -- it seemed a little interesting. In a normal environment I might have been more suspicious, but everyone was suspicious around here.

"Hurry up let's go," she said again, and began undressing in the cab as I drove down the street.

I was concerned about her scary enthusiasm, and watched with caution as she threw her slip over the seat. Whatever the scam was—I was going to turn it around.

"What's your name again?" I asked.

"Hey, I'm Lady G."

"You're a little wild."

"I'm from Viet Nam."

"That explains something, ...maybe."

Her bra flew over the seat. I looked at it suspiciously.

I could have been strangled. She was up to something other than what I might want, and it was time to take control.

"Hey, Lady G, I've been thinking of putting together an advertisement for the cab company with a picture of a naked girl sitting on the meter. It's hard to get cab drivers to drive a cab in Stockton, and maybe that would get some guys to want to drive taxi."

"That's a great idea!" She said; "You're smart."

"Well, I've got a camera in the trunk."

"Alright!" she yelled. "Give me three dollars."

I grabbed the camera and got in the backseat as Lady G, completely naked by now, was attempting to sit on the taxi meter -- just down the street from Mariani's, two blocks from the police station, in broad daylight.

I didn't think it could be done. But I got 2 pictures, one quite obscene, & hastily put the camera away while *Lady G* was buttoning her blouse. As soon as she was dressed I handed her three dollars; she snatched it, and abruptly jumped out of the cab without another word said.

Lady G disappeared in between two buildings in an area that was once considered Chinatown -- but now was being absorbed by the ever-increasing territory of the downtown drug markets. Descendents of Chinese who had worked on the railroad, or had been here for the gold rush, still lived in the area. Lady G didn't belong, but probably used it to blend in. Whatever Lady G was up to ... my short encounter was some scary fun.

Later that evening, I drove down the street where I imagined Lady G might still be hiding in the bushes, like a tiger laying wait. I didn't see her around, but I saw another woman waving. She looked Chinese, and probably not from Stockton -- standing in the street waving like that. I pulled up, she entered the cab, and I determined that she was a new immigrant from China. While driving down the block I tried to find out where she wanted to go. She spoke in broken English.

"Da ryte," she said.

I made a right turn.

She suddenly went ballistic; "Da ryte, da ryte …on top."

Was that a question? She was very agitated about it.

"Da ryte!" she said louder.

I knew very little Chinese, and her command of English wasn't working, but I still had to try to communicate: "Ling, Yi, eR, san, Su, wU, leeO.

"1,2,3,…" she said, with a subdued chuckle, and seemed to calm down for a moment; but I still needed to find out where she wanted to go, and wasn't getting close to an answer. She went back to her original communication -- about the light, or turning right, or the name of some place.

"Da ryyte," she said, attempting better enunciation.

"Where do you want to go?" I asked. "What are you talking about?" She didn't understand the question.

"Da ryte," she said, matter-of-factly. Then she asked; "Is this taxi?"

"Yes, this is taxi?" I replied, feeling that we were finally making a connection, but then she continued to spaz out;

"Da ryt... on top... is this taxi?"

I didn't answer, and she let out a sigh of frustration or

disgust. We had made it about 6 blocks in a direction away from Downtown or Mariani's, and toward the historic Wong Mansion—as reasonable assumption as any.

"How ah." She said.

"What?"

"Okay," she said, and waved her hand, pointing at the curb.

I didn't know if we had arrived where she wanted to go, or she had just given up. She was better distanced from trouble, so I considered it a successful failure and dropped her off.

I drove down the street without an idea of where to go next, and at this point didn't even want to check out the Greyhound station. As it got later in the evening they lock the front door of the Greyhound by the taxi stand. Whenever a bus came, the customers couldn't see a cab available if it was in front of the station. Security at the station made conducting business a problem.

The late-night security guard was quite a bully, and when taxi's came around to the back of the station to try to greet customers, the security guard would chase the taxi's away, claiming that the taxi stand in front was where they were supposed to be parking. I wasn't in the mood to deal with it and just drove around town aimlessly.

Late in the night, after having little luck scanning the streets, I rolled up beside a bus full of passengers heading for the Greyhound -- perhaps my last chance to get a decent fare for the night. I decided to follow it to the station. As I watched the bus pull into the lot I noticed the security guard -- shaking his finger and hollering at another cab driver. I pulled up, hoping that I could quickly get a fare while the bus was unloading, but in less than a minute the guard looked over at me, pointed his finger, and started to approach my cab. He started screaming about his interpretation of what it's like to drive a cab -- he knew all about it -- but the more he said, the more I realized he was just out of his mind.

"Please, you don't have to shout at me," I said.

He continued yelling.

"I'm not arguing with you, not bothering you, and if you can't talk to me without shouting, then we aren't going to have a conversation," I said calmly.

He started yelling louder; "If I ask you a question you are going to answer. If I tell you to do something you're going to do it."

This guy was a real crazy animal. I needed to get away.

"You know your job," I said; "And I know my job, and I've got to get to work now, so maybe we can talk some other time." I proceeded to drive off of the Greyhound lot — since the guard said I wasn't supposed to be there.

He became enraged; "You're not going anywhere when I'm talking."

Just as I was pulling out onto the street, the guard ran ahead of my driver window and punched me in the face.

A felony assault, and he broke my glasses. This was too much--somebody had to stop this abusive security guard, and the Greyhound should buy me a new pair of glasses.

I drove across the street to the police station. I told the receptionist that the security guard at Greyhound had just assaulted me when my car was in motion.

"Oh, not him again," the receptionist said; "Hang on,

and I'll get an officer."

I felt relieved that someone at the police station already knew the guard was a problem, and was glad to wait for an officer. I waited for quite awhile. Officers finally arrived and took my story, and then went across the street to talk to the security guard. The officers came back a few minutes later and told me that the security guard claimed that I had called him a nigger, and he was just defending himself.

"What?" I said in surprise; "I didn't call him anything, didn't want to try to talk to him at all, and left in order to avoid a confrontation."

Then the officer said; "I don't want to bother… if you want me to make a police report I'll write in big block letters that you called him a nigger, & the DA will just throw it out."

These were new officers who'd come from out of town for the money, I guessed, and understandably didn't relate to Stockton, and didn't want to bother with whatever my problem was. To help me with my problem, or not, their paycheck would be the same either way.

Just a year earlier, when I came to Stockton; officers who seemed very courteous and conscientious impressed me, and this was something new. Evidently, they upped the ante to hire more officers, and it turned to shit. More pay doesn't necessarily mean better workers.

With no glasses I couldn't see to read street signs, but I had the streets memorized anyway.

I found a couple of fares, and as I raced down the road to squeeze a little more time out of the night, I joked to my customers; "I can't see a damn thing." They all thought I was kidding. I could see well enough to come up with $50 before I went home to look for a spare pair of glasses.

The next day was a beautiful day – obscured only slightly by a scratch on some old glasses I found. The scratchy old glasses would have to do. I pulled out of the taxi lot and called to the dispatcher; "Where am I going?" I asked, to find out what position I could get into in the various zones. It was a big question to myself, because I usually went to the Greyhound.

"Four Central, second East, first North," said the dispatcher.

Central Stockton had the most business -- with a lot of bars, the train station, the downtown drug trade, and of course the Greyhound. Three other cabs were probably sitting at the Greyhound, but I wasn't stopping there.

I was disturbed about changing my habit. I decided to not change too much, and would find something else to do downtown. I called back to the dispatcher; "Four Central." I proceeded downtown—feeling lost.

"Alright, 79, you're #4."

Severely irritated as I drove down the street, I had to come to terms. It may be true that if we think bad things will happen, they will – so, to dwell on misfortune can only magnify it. I had to stop the rage and find a new direction.

I remembered the repetitive claims of the top gun fighter pilot, Rudel – '*He is lost who gives himself up for lost.*'

... And, W. C. Stone, who said:

'*Every adversity has an equal or greater benefit.*'

If only I could find that elusive benefit.

If I couldn't think positive about the situation, perhaps I shouldn't think about it at all. I tried to kick out the irritating thoughts-- think of something else.

It was time to try to turn bad into good, and I refreshed myself with thoughts of *The Power of Positive Thinking*. The feeling of defeat lifted when I thought of how comfortable my old glasses were, and that the scratch wasn't so bad. When I saw that the other three cabs were sitting at the Greyhound -- I could hope that they all get fares off of the bus, and make me 1st Central for radio call. I went to Mariani's to wait.

Posting up alongside the crowd by Mariani's -- I had wanted to turn bad into good, but it looked all bad around there. There was no cabstand of course, so I just double-parked with my flashers on, and acted like I was doing something I was supposed to be doing.

After sitting there awhile I noticed Jose behind the crowd. He was crouched in a doorway sucking a crack pipe. This is why I probably didn't notice him before. The time that he worked at my house was just after he got out of jail, and perhaps the longest period of time that he was clean. I hadn't noticed him because he always had been hiding in a doorway with the pipe.

As I watched, I realized how I had become important to him, and why he pestered me so much -- because for a moment I had given him hope for a way out. Jose really had some good qualities, but he was caught up in a dysfunctional family system within what appeared, overall, to be a dysfunctional society. He really didn't have a choice but to be fucked up.

Jose was smoking crack with Benjamin Cruz. I watched from a safe distance. Then Ben punched Jose in the face. I didn't see why, but right after being socked, Jose continued to try to puff the pipe. Then Ben snatched it away from him. They continued smoking crack amidst the fuss, and my perusal remained unnoticed.

A haunting thought pulsated: The social system that would help these people to find something else to do, wasn't there, or wasn't working. The prison workers, clerks, police, and prosecutors, and other people, will insist that the system works, regardless of even the most obvious failures.

Oh, it works for them... They'd never confess that the operations constitute a dysfunctional system, because they cope with it, and it rewards them generously. They even exist to try to force it on others. In the Justice system you can go to jail. In the educational system you can get an "F". And even when it's obvious that the system doesn't really work, there is no option but to go along.

There are dysfunctional systems everywhere that *pretend* to be functioning well. What else is there to do but to do what you're doing? All these people aren't going to give up their jobs, no matter how wicked, silly, or ineffective they are. Any wrong move and the whole system can be thrown into turmoil.

We needed this justice system to deal with people like Benjamin Cruz, but they weren't going to do a damned thing for Benjamin Cruz. The fucked up system would make him worse. Jose was lucky to get punched in the face by Ben, and perhaps be encouraged to not hang around him. Not knowing yet what their future had in store for them, I sat in the cab, looking at a crowd—none of what I witnessed looked like there was a future for these people to look forward to.

Finally, someone walked up to the cab and asked to go to a bar. I didn't tell the dispatcher about the pickup… I could keep my position for a radio call, because no other cabs were around to see me, and snitch. I took a guy a few blocks away for a quick $5.

I went back around to Mariani's, and the moment I pulled up some guy jumped in. He pointed down the street, and said; "Go up here."

I started driving without knowing where he wanted to go, which often turns out to be a bad idea, but I did it anyway. On the next block the guy tried to strong-arm rob me, with the cab in motion, just as we were passing the police station. I abruptly spun the wheel to the left; cars behind me slammed on their brakes, and I slid right over into the police patrol unit entrance. The guy jumped out of the cab without getting anything. I tried to find an officer, and finally got an officer's attention only to have him holler:

"Get the Hell out. Don't ever pull into this driveway."

I proceeded straight through the patrol vehicle staging area, and out the driveway facing the Greyhound station.

I had neglected to call into the dispatcher, of course -- not telling her I picked up a fare in the cuts on the sly.

It had been a while, and I had the radio turned down, so I may have been dropped from the list. As I pulled away from the police station I figured it was time to call in. I turned up the switch and keyed the mike; "79 is vacant at the Greyhound."

I was driving right through the Greyhound lot with the security guard looking at me hotly when the dispatcher responded: "79! Where have you been?"

"Someone was trying to rob me and I got distracted."

"What?"

"Never mind," I said, as I whipped it and did a donut in the Greyhound lot.

"What are you doing 79? ... Get Dameron."

"Check."

"Oh, I give up," said the dispatcher, "Just get Dameron, main entrance."

In line with the spirit of a bobcat, I was off to the next curiosity without regard to the trouble I'd left behind.

In a few minutes I was at Dameron hospital. An elderly woman who had taken a ride with me before was waiting at the main entrance. I opened the door and helped her in with her oxygen tank.

"Oh, I'm glad it's you," she said. "Some of these drivers are so nasty, and the cab is so filthy -- the company must be proud to have good drivers like you."

"Tell them that next time you call. You can ask for me if you wish."

"That would be wonderful. I can do that?"

"Sure, but they might think it's a prank call."

"What?" she asked, with a confused look.

"Oh, nothing," I said laughing, "Where would you like to go today?"

"You know, Casa Manana."

"Oh, that's right," I said, but I didn't know. As we drove off, I called the dispatcher; "79 en route to Casa Manana."

"Thank you, 79."

"Boy," I said to myself out loud, "The company should be proud."

"What?" asked the customer.

"Oh, nothing, I was just talking to myself."

"Yeah, well, I'll go to Saint Joseph's next time," the customer informed me.

"Really," I said; "Why's that?"

"They keep you waiting forever in there. You could die in the waiting room."

"Yep, you'd be a skeleton before they got to you," I said jokingly.

"Right," she said, "And then they just sent me home and I really don't feel right. I shouldn't go home."

"Yes ma'am, I understand, things aren't the way people think they ought to be."

"Really, I'm sick of these doctors," she said, "I was at another hospital and they wanted to take my leg off, but I wanted to get a second opinion first, and was complaining a whole bunch about it ...and that doctor ...you know what he told me?" She asked, as she looked at me wide-eyed.

"What did he say?" I asked

That doctor said; "Hey, you can be eliminated."

"Really?" I said, holding back a laugh.

"Yeah! That's what he said. You know how much these doctors make for snatching a leg?"

"No," I said.

"The insurance pays for it - about $25,000."

"Well," I said. "I guess that's an incentive to do a few amputations."

"Huh! But I'd like to amputate that doctors head," she said, making a slash with her hand.

"Ooo boy, you've got a spirit in ya'."

"That's a fact, and I'm 83 years old."

"Well, if you were just a little younger I'd have to make you my gal," I said jokingly.

She got a kick out of that, and we sat and talked in front of the Casa Manana about doctors, and the cab service for a few more minutes.

I called in to the dispatcher; "79 is vacant."

"Two central." said the dispatcher, placing me in position for a radio call with just one other cab ahead of me downtown.

I proceeded to scour the streets to look for something to do while waiting for another order. A few minutes later Mean Marion was calling in your usual scolding tone; "79!"

"Yes," I responded.

"You have a complaint, and they are threatening to sue."

"What? Who?" I asked.

"The Lady's husband says you were detaining her in the cab trying to flirt with her, and he's mad as hell."

"What lady? What husband? You got the right driver?"

"Yes, I've got the right driver!" she said with a tone of childish sarcasm, "You had her over by Casa Manana."

"Marion, that lady lives in the Casa Manana retirement home, and she's 83 years old, so get off it."

"Oh well, whatever, you'd just better watch it, and don't screw this next one up ... get Saint Joseph's..."

"OK," I said.

"Wait, 79, and pay attention; Go to the third floor lab and get some aneurysm clips for Dameron emergency right away, and don't give me this check stuff."

I paused for a moment, thinking... Huh, she wants me to repeat back the order?

I responded accordingly; "Saint Joseph's, third floor, find aneurysm clips, bring to Dameron emergency."

"Alright, I think you've got it, charge it to Dameron."

Saint Joseph's hospital was just a few blocks away. I hit the meter and parked at the emergency entrance. I walked through the main lobby, took the elevator, and wandered around the third floor. The whole time, I didn't see a soul at the hospital; there was just expensive hospital equipment with nobody in attendance. Finally, down a long hall I found a nurse who was startled to see me.

"City Cab here to pick up some aneurysm clips for Dameron." I announced.

"Oh, let me see if I can find out something for you." I followed her as she walked back to the lab mumbling something to herself about aneurysm clips.

We made it back to the reception area, and she invited me to watch TV while she found out about my delivery order.

The 10 o'clock news was just starting. I sat to watch halfway through the frightening display of nonsense that bombarded me from the electronic menace.

A guard appeared. "What are you doing here?" he asked, with a heavy foreign accent.

"Watching the news while I'm waiting for aneurysm clips."

"Is that a patient?" he demanded gruffly.

"What? Aneurysm clips?"

"Yes, is that a patient?" he asked, with an attitude like he was about to make an arrest.

"Oh yeah, my Auntie Aneurysm," I spit back. "Ms. Clips should be here by now. No really, I'm just kidding, I think it's a medical device that I have to deliver to Dameron."

"Oh," he said, in a more friendly tone; "Why didn't you tell me?"

"I did, and I've been waiting quite a while for the nurse to return with the device."

The guard got on his radio. I ignored him until he left a few minutes later. I watched the news until it was over, and had wasted over 45 minutes by the time the nurse finally appeared again.

"It's about time!"

"Sorry," she said, "We found them, but now they don't need them anymore."

"All right, thanks," I said, as I pushed the elevator button -- thinking maybe the patient had died.

Marion was off her shift, and I had trouble explaining to the relief dispatcher what had transpired; "I was supposed to deliver to Dameron and charge them, but I was tied up by Saint Joseph's for 45 minutes only to find out that the delivery order was canceled, so who do I charge?"

After a long pause the dispatcher responded; "Charge Saint Joseph's for waiting time, 79."

"Who signs the charge tag?"

"Never mind, we'll take care of it, just tell me how much is on the meter."

"Alright, how about 27.50 ... and where am I?"

"I don't know where you are. You can be third central."

"Check" and I'm at Saint Joseph's."

"You're third central, or second east."

"Third central."

"Alright 79."

Weeding through the confusion with the dispatcher sometimes seemed to never end. I was glad to hang up the radio mic, and also glad to see the image of Saint Joseph's grow smaller in my rear-view mirror until it disappeared.

I wasn't driving anywhere in particular, just driving, but then my attention was captured when I stopped at a signal light and noticed a young girl waiting for the bus. When I looked in her face time stopped. She was real cute, just what I thought cute should be. What a lucky cowboy would be waiting to greet her every day. How much I wished that this girl standing on the street corner would be mine.

I was spoiled by the convenience of having about a half dozen girlfriends. Yet, with an abundance of willing women at hand I had a feeling ... here was a gal worth leaving all the others behind.

She wasn't like any of the girls you'd see out on the town. We were a few blocks away from the area where the wicked women strolled, and she was definitely not one of them -- she was something special.

I felt jealous of her imagined boyfriend.

Just then she stuck out her thumb.

Wow, I waved her to come on.

"I don't have any money, I was trying to hitchhike," she said, as she opened my taxi door rather shyly.

"Get in!" I said.

She had beautiful silky brown hair, and dark brown eyes, richly alive and inviting. She was like a little charm -- a short girl less than 5 feet tall.

"My name is Caitlin," she said, as she hopped into the front seat.

"What's a girl like you doing out here at night? Where's the old man, how come he doesn't come and pick you up?"

"Oh, he's an asshole."

"Where's he at right now?"

"I don't know -- haven't seen him in a long time."

"Well, where do you want to go? I'll take you home."

I felt like I might be getting somewhere, certainly she was getting somewhere -- she was getting a free ride. And I definitely wanted to know where she lived.

"You'll take me, really? I live all the way over on Country Club."

"Oh yeah, sure, I think there's a cab stand over that way." There's going to be one in front of her house, I thought.

"Hey, that's really cool," she said, smiling. I nearly fainted when she smiled at me. She sat there smiling as I drove her way across town. I felt like it wasn't far enough. I would've liked to drive around the world. Then she said; "I take cabs a lot, can I ask for you?"

"Oh, yes you can!" I handed her a business card, and then another business card before I dropped her off. Then I drove around for more than an hour without a hint of a fare, but I didn't care. I wasn't going to make any money, but felt rich for meeting a special girl. It was the next to last day of the month, and the night held little prospects for making money, yet I got lucky in another way, so why beat a dead horse to make a buck? I decided to rush home and spank the monkey.

The next day I started early, and usually the early part around the shift change is busy for a little while, but I drove around for nearly an hour without a fare. The dispatcher knew that I wasn't having any luck, and out of mercy, I imagined, offered me a call: "79, you wanna go North?"

"I want to go somewhere," I replied.

"Get 1460 Bradford Street, and go up to the door."

Evidently, the last driver failed to get a customer, because he just honked the horn and no one responded. So, it might not be a blessing. Somebody none of the other drivers wanted to pick up; Or there will be nobody there at all. Even on a dead slow night some drivers dump calls. Sometimes several calls would come out for the same address, because the drivers found something there that they just didn't like. The way to avoid an argument with the dispatcher was to claim they couldn't find the customer, or; as odd as claims of shark attacks on Main Street, the taxi driver would claim he got lost.

In reality they were scared -- but drivers are responsible for their own safety, so whatever the reason, driver discretion couldn't be contested.

Various idiosyncrasies had to be included. One of the drivers had a social anxiety disorder, and was subject to panic attacks, so the dispatcher would call out to him sometimes; "Slow down to 40 miles per hour so the customers might jump on your fenders."

Whatever the reason, some people just had to call back twice, and that's just the way it was. I tried harder than a lot of drivers, and assumed that I had a customer until I was really proven wrong. If there was a fare I was going to find it. Bradford Street wasn't that hard to find, and I wondered what kind of surprise I had in store for me.

I pulled up in front of the house and went to the door. I rang the bell and knocked, and heard a voice from inside, an angry voice; "Come in."

I don't normally like to go into strange places, and always wait for someone to come to the door. I could hear that the bell worked, and rang it again. The angry voice became louder, swearing, and demanding; "...come in, come in." It sounded like a drunken elderly woman, and many cabdrivers would've claimed to be lost if asked to find such things. The most difficult customers that you might ever encounter -- other than the ones that want to kill you – are drunken old women. Then I heard her holler; "Please help me!" I open the door slightly, peered in through the crack, and saw a one-legged elderly woman sitting on a couch.

"Hey, the door's unlocked!" she yelled, in a hostile voice; "And don't lock it behind you when you leave, because somebody else did, and it took me three days to get to the door to unlock it so someone else could come in to help me. Would you please come in and sit down?!"

This was starting to not make sense, but I had learned to be patient, not jump to conclusions, and even to question whatever conclusions I came to. We might think it was a crank call by a crazy old lady that had too much to drink... but what? She seemed to have something really important to say, and she was fuming mad.

I didn't want to sit down and talk. "I sit all night in the cab, and I'd rather stand, please." I said, still standing by the door.

"Well, then stand there and listen." Her tone calmed down, and she nearly choked on her words as she continued; "I want to ask you to do me a favor."

"What's that?" I asked.

"Pick me up and take me to bed."

I paused, as my right foot impulsively inched back toward the exit.

I could see the headlines now on a tabloid at the supermarket: *Weird Cabbie Takes Old One Legged Woman to Bed in a Rape Attack*. She wanted me to pick her up and take her to bed? We have to be careful about how we word things nowadays. I'd been accused of enough absurdity by witch-hunt wanting fools. People believe in nonsense: If a bird took a crap on a statue at just the right spot and it dripped down the eye -- thousands of believers would travel for miles to see the Holy statue that shed a tear. I'm scared of such people. And those same kind of people would be tryin' to find something wrong with the situation with this old lady. My mind wandered nervously. Then the woman went on to explain:

"I had a regular cab driver for awhile," she said; "and I'd give him five dollars to carry me from my bed to the couch, and another five dollars to come back before he got off his shift to take me back to bed."

So, it appeared to me that this wasn't normal taxi service -- but transportation services between a couch and a bed. The Lady seemed very angry, and frustrated, but her anger wasn't really directed at me. I sat down to hear her story. She explained that taxi service seemed to serve her the best, but it didn't always work. In the past, out of desperation she had called police and fire services, but got into a little trouble for that. She had called for pizza delivery, just to see if she could get someone to help her with her struggles in life -- getting back and forth between a bed and the couch to watch TV.

I saw a wheelchair; "What about that?"

"I can grab it and hop to the bathroom, but it's very difficult for me to get up, and if I sit in that wheelchair I'm more or less stuck. I had a helper for a while, but now they only come by twice a week to do the laundry, make me something to eat and wash the dishes...

...There aren't many dishes to do, because I only struggle to hop to the kitchen once in awhile to make something to eat for myself, and often end up crawling when I try that."

We talked for about an hour, and the angry women had plenty to be angry about. Her name was Val, and she explained that her leg had been amputated without her permission, and that she should have been allowed to get a second opinion. She was a very intelligent woman, and rather articulate, elaborating on the errors of the medical system, and how its most effective function was to enrich doctors. She told stories about other kinds of elder abuse, and of helplessness. She had a wonderful life at one time, and had been the general manager of a major department store -- only to end up living a life traversing an 18 ft. trail, and a daily dose of Valium.

I had heard many similar complaints before. To me, her story was not very unusual, just overlooked. "I'd like to be able to do something about all of this," I said.

"Would you try?" she asked.

"I always am." I replied.

"Don't give up." she said.

"For now, I really need to get back to work."

"Well, I've been sitting on the couch for three days. I managed to crawl to the door and unlock it this morning, and have been trying all day to get someone to come and help... I would like to pay you five dollars to just carry me over and put me in my bed."

"That's fine, and you call me anytime you want, Val."

"Thanks," she said, holding out a five-dollar bill.

"OK, you want to pay the fare in advance, I said with a laugh. Tell me how I need to pick you up."

I carried her into the adjoining room and gently placed her on her bed. I left the house as she yelled; "Make sure you don't lock the door."

Walking back to the cab I didn't know if I was happy to help, or saddened because I had to.

I left Bradford Street, wondering what kind of night I would have, and wasn't encouraged. A woman flagged me down as I drove through downtown, but as I pulled over she walked away from me, and started to run up some stairs.

"Hey, do you want a cab?" I hollered.

"Yes, I do," she said, as she turned to continue up the stairs.

"But… you are walking away from me -- when do you want a cab?"

"Right now," she said, glancing over her shoulder.

"Then where are you going? If you want me to wait -- how long?"

"Yes," she said anxiously, still trying to go somewhere else other than to the cab.

"Yes what? When do you want this cab? I'm ready."

"I need a cab right now, on the corner down a block."

"You are going up into that building, and you want a cab a block away…when?"

"Right now, she said again, and disappeared into the building."

I didn't want to wait around to try to find out how long 'right now' was. This woman could easily become someone

I'd just have to kick out of the cab whenever 'right now' arrived, anyway. It seemed to be a regional peculiarity that in Stockton 'right now' was a universal unit of time which could in reality be anywhere from 3 minutes to 3 days.

Even though it was a slow night I knew better than to wait, and would find something else to do.

Two hours into the shift I had but five dollars in hand, the radio was quiet, and there was no way I was going around the Greyhound.

The only thing that the last day of the month had to offer was looking forward to the excitement of the first of the month. There was nothing to do but wait. I could hope to break even, but otherwise how would I waste the night? Worse than silence, the radio gave off an annoying buzz, unbearable for so long, but I had to listen. Finally it crackled with the dispatchers voice; "79, you have a personal, Country Club and I-5." She knew I was listening, but I didn't answer back -- I was too concerned about a quick maneuver to a nearby freeway on-ramp. It was that girl -- she called after all.

Once positioned on the freeway I grabbed the microphone; "79."

The dispatcher responded; "79, you have a personal. Country Club and I-5 at the gas station."

In just three minutes I was pulling off of the freeway and could see Caitlin at the gas station on the corner.

"Hey," she said, cheerfully, "I told you I'd call. I've got money this time, too. I'll give you $20 to give me a ride downtown and back."

"That's great, do people call you Kate?"

"No, my name starts with a 'C', so they call me Cat, but I spell it with a 'K'."

"KK...Kat?"

"Something like that."

"But your name is with a 'C'."

"Yes, that's me."

Our conversation went on in rhyme as I headed back to the freeway on-ramp.

We seemed to hit it off so perfectly, but I didn't know anything, so I asked rather bluntly; "Tell me about your life."

"Well, I'm from the Bay Area."

"Me too, I used to drive taxi in San Francisco."

"I used to hang around Powell Street with my girlfriend."

"When was that?"

"In the eighties, we lived on Haight Street."

"I lived at Haight & Steiner," I revealed.

"We lived at Haight & Pierce."

"You lived a block away from me?"

"Yeah, I guess so. My roommate had a crush on the guy who lived over at Haight & Steiner, but it wasn't you -- his name was Kevin."

"Really, did you ever go over there?"

"No, but my roommate was nuts about Kevin."

"Yeah, I knew Kevin, I said. You don't remember me at Haight & Steiner?"

"No, I knew Kevin, but never went where he stayed."

"How long did you stay on Haight Street?" I asked.

"A couple of years, and then I moved to 465 Lexington in Hayward after my roommate broke a lamp over my head."

"What...?" Curious about the lamp incident, but more

curious about her move from Haight Street to 465 Lexington – apparently at about the time I moved to 465 Grove in Hayward. "What did you do in Hayward?" I asked.

"I got a job at a music store in the mall."

"There was a piano store in the mall, you didn't work there, did you?" I asked. (It was where I worked at the time.)

"No, it was a record store across from the piano store."

Wow, I wondered if it was her; One day, when I bought a music book at that record store, and wished that I knew what it would take to get a girl like that cashier... as she totally ignored me in the process of ringing up my purchase. I didn't tell Cat about the coincidences that were unfolding.

"How did you come to Stockton?" I asked.

"I found out the rent was cheap, and got a job as an administrative assistant working in an office."

I had more-or-less done the same thing. This was amazing. And somehow we both ended up being out on the streets at night. But what was she doing? She was dropping off some papers to a girl downtown -- something to do with social services. She explained her situation:

"I only work part-time now, because I've got an ordeal with traffic court that interferes with getting a full-time job."

I was totally swept away. I assumed that she worked part-time for a paralegal, or social worker, but didn't ask. She wanted to go to Mariani's to drop of papers, and I thought nothing of it -- she acted so professional.

A small crowd of dope fiend's lurked around the stairway of an old residential hotel. Cat got out of the cab, pushed her way through the crowd, and ran up the flight of stairs with a manila envelope full of papers in her hand. I could admire a brave woman -- especially one who would put herself in such a position in order to help someone else.

I was still speechless when I dropped her off again at Country Club and I-5. She told me that she was going out of town for a week, and said that she would call me when she came back. I had yet to tell her about our coincidences. She still really knew nothing about me-- I was sure --but she had to know that we might have something special going on. She was my Brunhilde.

I drove away wondering if she would ever even call back, or how many days really were in a week. Parallel lives, a perfect match, and so beautiful to me -- I had no idea what was in store, or how treacherous the next parallel could turn out to be. My surprises were just beginning. I could only imagine perfection. What if I didn't see her again? I could only wish a week had fewer days.

It was approaching eight o'clock, and I only had $25. I needed three times that much just to be comfortably broke. I called into the dispatcher; "79 is vacant on Country Club." I was lucky; two cabs were posted in the north, both were busy, and another order had just come in.

"Do you want to get Lyons, 79?"

The customer was usually gone by the time a cab got there for some reason, but it was worth a try. I tried to joke with the ornery dispatcher. "Did you say you're a lion? Or I'm lying?"

"You'll be lyin' on the floor when I get my hands on you, 79."

"The restaurant?"

"Right, you got Lyons on Pacific Avenue."

"Alright, thanks."

"79, do you have the order?"

"Check."

"79, repeat the order."

"OK, Lyons in the restaurant."

"You got it."

I pulled up to Lyons restaurant and a guy was standing in the parking lot, smoking. He got in the cab, and asked to go to the Greyhound station. I joked around with him about it:

"Oh shit, you want to take a Greyhound bus?"

"Yeah, you're right," he said, as he laughed and coughed.

"And you can't smoke on the bus."

"Yeah," he said, still coughing.

"You can't smoke or drink, and you'll need a drink on that horrible bus ride. The fat lady in front of you will be spraying her hair, and you'll get hairspray in your face; and then her baby will start screaming."

The guy was laughing.

"Where are you taking the bus to?"

"Up to Reno to gamble."

"The Greyhound sounds like bad luck, take a cab, it'll bring you luck."

He started laughing harder.

I continued, "You're gonna lose the money anyway, but I'll take you half price. How long were you planning on staying up there?"

"Just two or 3 hours to gamble."

"Perfect -- sounds like a lucky cab ride, and you won't be waiting around for the bus to bring you back broke... Yes, a quick trip in the cab will bring you luck. OK... $125 for the ride, and $50.00 to wait 2 hours, and I'll gamble too -- and you can smoke and drink all the way." I was joking, but I was serious, too.

"I'll probably lose the money anyway, and I could use a beer," he said; "What the heck, pull over at that liquor store."

How cool that he took my joke seriously... I collected $175 in advance, and by midnight we were in Reno. By 3 AM I had spent $50 on keno tickets and cocktails, and my customer had won $280 at the crap table. I reminded him that we were only supposed to stay two hours, and it had been three -- and a good time to quit while he was ahead.

"Sure, I made back more than what it costs for the cab ride, and it's great that I don't have to fuck with the bus. Let's go."

"Yeah, fuck the bus," I said.

Riding back in a taxicab made the customer feel like more of a winner, and he offered to fill my gas tank when we got back to Stockton. I made it just in time to turn in the cab at the deadline. It turned out to be a good night by surprise – that's usually how it goes, you never know.

The first of the month rolled around as if a checkered flag was waving wildly. The race was on to spend the welfare checks.

There was such a huge demand for taxi service that some people would wait for hours-- and then they tried to keep the cab on waiting time as they made several stops. Waiting time cut into profits, and the people weren't going to tip, so... the customers that were somewhat unpleasant had to pay up front, and we'd negotiate the price.

The first few days of the month were especially

demanding work -- it was also my best chance to have a good month, so I had to make sure to keep busy. Some people would hold the cab, and by the time they made several stops around town, buying groceries or whatever -- their entire check was spent, and of course; with the last stop being at Mariani's.

This month I did well on the first three days, and by the fourth of the month I had enough to pay almost all my bills. I just needed a little more for the phone and food -- and it was a good thing, because business was starting to wind down. If I had a good night I'd be set for the month.

I pulled out from taxi lot feeling confident. Some people got checks on the third, and usually it stayed busy until the fifth. After the fifth it turned into something horrible, with a little relief on the 15th. I drove towards downtown speculating on how my success would be for the night. I had neglected to call in to the dispatcher to peg a position in an area for service, but the dispatcher had seen me leave and all the other cabs were busy...

She called me over the radio; "79?"
"Yes ma'am."
"What are you doing?"
"What do you want me to do?"
"Get the Trucadero."

The Trucadero was a popular bar located at the geographic center of the California Street drug trade.

A heroin dealer might be sitting at the bar, or a patron could be holding drugs for a dealer outside. Most of the people were there just to drink, and aside from the frenzy going on in front of the place, it was just a popular bar.

It was early in the evening, and the usual mob had not yet converged on the streets. As I pulled up in front of the place there were only a couple dozen people lingering on the block. I pushed through the double doors and yelled at the bartender; "Taxi!" The bartender pointed at a woman at the end of the bar, who in turn raised her hand.

I walked across the bar to scrutinize the customer where she sat, and leave her sitting there if it didn't look good.

As I approached her the bartender called her 'Virginia' while placing a shopping bag with two six-packs of beer on the bar in front of her. The name 'Iris' was embroidered on her blouse. I didn't ask her name. She looked a little tipsy, but good to go, so I asked her where she was headed.

"Greyhound," she said

"Oh no, they won't let you on the bus with two six-packs of beer -- they won't even ask to see how well you can walk a straight line. You might not be very drunk, but you're a little drunk, and you won't be riding the bus tonight."

"That's right," said the bartender, "They won't let you on the bus if you've been drinking, and you can't take beer onboard."

"Well, it's legal to drink in the backseat of the cab," I said, "And a cab can go anywhere the bus can go -- Where are you trying to get to?"

"Visalia."

"That would be an expensive cab ride, but you could drink all the way --And you're not taking the bus anywhere."

"How much?"

"Oh, it would be a lot – what'll you give me?"

She cocked her head and gave me a tough lookover. She was a rugged woman who looked like she had worked all of her life tossing sacks of cement, and was poised to be a big shot with that look, it seemed, but continued to sit there without saying anything.

"Well, you can go to a motel or somewhere else, but if you want to go to Visalia, make me an offer -- you're not going to take the bus."

She squinted her eye and cocked her head a little further as she held up four fingers.

"$400?" I asked.

She nodded slightly.

"That's a lot of money, but it's a discount for what the fare should be. You have to pay in advance."

"I'll pay on the way."

"OK, if you want to do it -- let's go."

Virginia loaded her two six-packs of beer into the back of the cab. I called her Virginia, and she never said anything different. She popped a beer open before I even pulled away from the curb as we headed off towards the freeway. I waited until we were approaching the on-ramp... "Alright Virginia, we're on our way, and you have to pay the fare in advance."

"I'll give it as we go," she said, handing me $100 bill over the seat.

"Why do you want to do it that way?"

"I just do."

"OK, you have to give me another hundred dollars when we get to Manteca."

She threw an empty beer can on the floor and popped another beer.

At Manteca I managed to collect a second hundred-dollar bill. Another 20 minutes later we were around

Modesto, and I was concerned about Virginia getting too drunk for me to collect the rest of the fare.

"Virginia, you need to pay the fare."

"Alright," she said, and handed me another hundred-dollar bill.

"When are you going to pay the rest of the fare?"

She seemed to look at me a little cross-eyed, then said: "When we get to Turlock."

"Hey," I demanded; "When we get to Turlock, that's far enough, and you can pay the rest of the fare, OK?"

She choked on the beer, and it ran down her chin. She didn't answer my question. I didn't know if she agreed. I just kept driving. In Turlock she wasn't responding very well. At least I had $300.

There were 12 empty beer cans scattered around on the floor of the cab as were approaching Merced. "Come on, Virginia, the last hundred dollars."

"I already gave it to you."

"No you didn't. You gave me $300 so far, and we agreed to 400."

"I gave you 400."

"No, you gave me 300, and I practically had to twist your arm to get it."

"Okaay."

Just as she stretched out her hand with the last hundred-dollar bill she spewed vomit all over the place.

I grabbed the $100 bill by the corner and held it carefully --dripping slime on the passenger side of the front seat.

We were just at a freeway off ramp, and I exited the freeway hoping I could find a place to clean up the mess.

I drove into Merced for about five minutes -- Virginia in

the backseat moaning. Finally I found a self-service carwash that looked desolate, and I could only hope that it was in working order. The car wash turned out to be operating, and with change in my pocket it looked like it might be a successful mission.

I turned to Virginia; "Alright, I know exactly what to do, but you have to get out of the cab." I helped Virginia out of the cab, and asked her to stand back. She staggered away a few feet as I used the power washer to spray all the puke off of the backseat. Then I took the car to the vacuum, and vacuumed up the water -- trying to dry the seats as much as possible.

"That's pretty good," said Virginia.

"Yep, I just spay out the interior of the car with the pressure washer and vacuum up the water -- it works good under these circumstances."

"Do that to me," said Virginia.

We had to do something, so I asked Virginia to stand in the middle of the carwash stall, and sprayed her off with the pressure washer. "I think it was in wax mode, Virginia, but that won't hurt anything -- maybe your dress will shine."

"At least I'm clean," said Virginia. She flung her arm in the air in a gesture of enthusiasm, and slipped and fell in the carwash stall.

I helped her up, and walked her over to a position where we could try to dry her off with the vacuum.

A purple Buick with 22-inch rims dipped and swerved and whipped around the corner just as I was applying the vacuum to Virginia's dress. The vacuum sucked Virginia's dress up in the air, and teenagers in the purple Buick started hanging out the window and hooting as they slowly scraped their way past the carwash.

"Hey Virginia, I think you've got a date."

Virginia didn't respond.

"Virginia, you're just going to have to drip dry, because the vacuum is not going to work on you."

"That's fine," she said. "At least I'm clean," and she started to fling her arm in the air again. I grabbed her arm to steady her just before she fell again, and helped her stagger back to the cab.

It wasn't long before we made it to Visalia. I helped Virginia get into a very modest house where she lived. She might have lost her whole paycheck, but at least she got home safely.

As I left, I wondered what Virginia's life was like. I felt a little grief for having had to charge her so much after seeing where she lived, but for what the cab fare should have been, she got a big discount -- as well as laundry service.

It was a long ride back to Stockton. Giving Virginia a ride home took up a good part of my shift, but I had $400, and it was very rare to book that much in one night. I could just turn in early and call it a good night, but I decided to pick up another fare if something was available. So, I called into the dispatcher as I was approaching Stockton on Highway 99...

"I've got a call over on Filbert," announced the dispatcher; "You wanna get it, 79?"

Filbert Street included an area that you really had to be careful about. I had $400 on me, but people who want to rob cabs generally don't call and wait for a cab to show up at a specific address. I didn't need to worry about it too much, and responded to the dispatcher; "All right, give me the call."

"OK 79, get 920 North Filbert -- for a lady."

That was good -- not the worst part of Filbert Street, and a woman. "920 Filbert, I'm on my way."

I pulled up in front of a rundown house surrounded by overgrown bushes that set adjacent to the railroad tracks. I wasn't going into the dark area behind the shrubbery to try to find the doorbell, and just honked the horn and waited in front. A couple minutes later a woman came out and got into the front seat of the cab, acting nervous. Then she pulled out a revolver and pointed at me, not saying anything. I sat there calmly, scrutinizing her and her gun. We continued to sit, silently, with her pointing the gun at me.

Taxi robbers usually get an average of only $50, but this girl hit the jackpot.

How was I going to get out of this?

I continued to sit there calmly -- concerned that she appeared to be getting agitated. She tried to say something, but just stuttered. I had better respond.

"Hey lady! Do you know what that is? That's a Saturday night special, and today is Tuesday. You'd better be careful, because that thing could blow up on you."

Her jaw dropped, and she just sat there, still silent.

"Alright, give me the gun," I said casually; "And I'll give you $10 and a ride to Mariani's and back."

"You will?" she asked.

"Yes," I said firmly; "Now give me the gun before you hurt yourself."

"You'll give me a ride back?"

"Yes," I said, as I grabbed the gun out of her hand and handed her a $10 bill. "And in the future don't pull guns out on people, because you don't know what you're doing."

"I know -- it was stupid." she said.

"I bet you could tell me all about stupid." I told her.

"What?" she look confused.

"Mariani's – What do you think is there?" I demanded.

"Stupid?" she asked.

"Never mind. When we get to Mariani's, just get out of the cab and do whatever you're doing away from me, and I'll sit and wait for you."

"Alright," she said.

I took the woman on her crack run, and then returned her to the shoddy house on Filbert Street. I decided that I'd had enough for one night and turned in the cab. It was the 5th time that I'd had someone pull a gun on me -- And I ended up with the gun each time. I wanted to keep this one as a trophy. It really was a junk Saturday night special, made in Miami, and barely a functional firearm.

The following day I found out that a week could mean five days -- Cat was back. I had been worried that she might disappear on me, and wondered if she realized what seemed obvious to me: That there was a special connection between us. The dispatcher informed me that Cat had called for me just a few minutes before I got to work. At least she was back. Now the only question was when would she call again.

Only six blocks away from the lot the dispatcher called to me over the radio; "79... Country Club and I-5."

I could tell that the dispatcher knew something was up, and probably figured that I wouldn't be heard from for a while. A good guess, because I had stacked up enough cash over the past few days, and the only business I was interested in at the moment was that girl.

I sped off to swoop her up.

Within minutes I was pulling off the freeway, and could see her at the gas station pacing around in white leather boots, wearing a red leather jacket.

"Hey, I was worried…"

"What, you didn't think I'd call?"

"Well, you might have decided not to come back to Stockton -- the place kind of sucks."

"You're right about that, but I did come back, and I'm glad to see you."

"Well, what are you trying to do right now?"

"I'm gonna go hang out with the girls and go barhopping."

"Oh yeah?"

"It's a little early, but I like drinking with my girlfriends, and there are a few people I haven't seen for awhile."

"So where are you going?"

"You can take me over to Pinchot and Wilson way."

"Are you in a hurry?"

"Not really, why?"

"I was wondering if I could take you and show you where I live."

"Sure, I've got time."

Shortly thereafter we pulled up in front of my house. "Come on, let me show you the place," I said.

Cat jumped out of the car and went up the stairs. She sat down on the porch rail looking real sexy. I went up the stairs and opened the door, inviting Cat in on a tour of the house. I watched her carefully for signs of approval. She seemed to show interest.

"That one eyed old man you've been staying with," I asked, "You don't have to stay there, do you?"

"No, I don't."

"Why don't you stay here with me tonight?"

"I've got plans to be out drinking with the girls until late."

"I usually work until 4 AM."

"That sounds good to me."

"But how will I find you?"

"I'll meet you -- come on, I'll show you where you can pick me up later." she said.

I drove her to Wilson Way & Pinchot.

"OK," she said; "This is good, and I can meet you later – right here."

"What time?"

"The bars close at 2 a.m., and I can meet you here at 3, or whenever."

"I can turn in the cab any time I want, and I want to spend some time with you, so 3 or even earlier will suit me."

"Well," she said, "I stay out 'till 4 a lot of the time, and I'm going to be out at least until the bars close. How about if I meet you at 3 right on this corner?"

"I'll be looking for you." I promised.

As I drove away I wondered who her girlfriends were, and what they were like. I had so many questions. We seemed like such a perfect match, and I wondered what she thought. I couldn't wait to spend more time with her. I spent the rest of the evening driving around just waiting until 3 AM arrived.

At 2:45 a.m. I parked the cab at Wilson & Pinchot, and waited until 3:15 -- no Cat. I drove around, searching the neighborhood, and repeatedly passed by the special corner where my girl was supposed to be. I was anxious to find her, but she wasn't to be found. I took a radio call and would check back later. I passed by the corner again after picking up a customer.

"Why are you going this way?" asked the customer

"I thought it would be easier." I replied.

The customer didn't ask any more, and didn't really seem to care much. After dropping the customer off I was back on the corner again at 3:50 a.m.. I drove around scanning each block in the vicinity, and returned to the corner for a look again, and again. It was 4:20 by the time I figured that I'd been stood up. I drove around a few more minutes -- not wanting to give up, but it was pointless. I turned in the cab and went home feeling depressed.

As I approach my house I noticed that the kitchen light was on, and the window slightly opened. The whole thing was a setup, I worried -- me on the corner at the same time my home was being robbed by some other boyfriend. I didn't really know her, and I suspected she was caught up with some bad people – not unlike my own habits, perhaps.

As I opened the front door I heard a scuffle. Certainly I had been burglarized. Someone was still inside.

That girl set me up.

I grabbed a stick that I kept by the door and crept quietly down the dark hallway.

Moving slowly, with only a narrow beam of light coming from the kitchen to break the darkness -- I pressed my left shoulder against the wall by the living room entrance, clutching a stick in my right hand ready to strike. Someone was in there. I peeked around the corner and could barely make out the shadow of a figure sitting on the couch.

"Is that you?" came a voice in the dark. It was Cat. She broke into my house? I reached over to turn on the light.

"So, you're a burglar?" I asked.

"Worse than that -- a rapist." She exclaimed.

As the light went on I saw that Cat was sitting there completely naked. She sprang from the couch and pounced on me, knocking me to the ground. She hissed and growled, then tore off my clothes. Perhaps I should have been alarmed by the way she played the role of a rapist, but at the moment I found it hilarious, and quite a thrill.

I didn't mind being raped at all. We rolled around on the carpet for a couple of hours, then fell asleep, cuddling naked on the living room floor.

The late morning sun shining through the window awakened me. Exhilarated, still holding Cat naked in my arms-- I felt like she was mine forever, already. It seemed too wonderful, and I wondered if it was really true. Then Cat opened her eyes and looked at me lovingly, as if to answer.

I kissed her as I moved my hand up her back, massaging her and turning her over to wrap my arms around her and hold her close.

"No other man has made me feel this way -- in fact I don't really like men…" As she said this I paused as if I had a question. "Until I found you," She added. If I had a question, I didn't know what the question was, and I wasn't about to allow suspicion to taint something so perfect.

"Hey, can I take you to breakfast or lunch?" I asked her.

"It's about time for either one, and I'm hungry enough

for both," she answered.

"What are you doing today -- and tonight? I've got the night off."

"I thought we were going to lunch?"

"Yes, lunch." I said, and shut up.

We both got dressed and headed out the door. At lunch it went on like she was someone I'd known for an eternity. Even the negative aspects were exciting to me -- she informed me that she had a drinking problem. Exciting to me because it was a problem to solve -- to rescue the damsel in distress, my princess. I dug into the issue, and she told of going to jail because of drinking, and described a childhood with an alcoholic mother, and an abusive father.

Cat said that her father abused her sexually, and beat her mother, and that's why her mother was mean, and a drunk.

She told of a time when she had been longing for her mother, and ran up to greet her at an airport. Cat had her arms outstretched, and her mother just pushed her away. She talked about her craving for affection from her mean alcoholic mother -- and this was a clue about something.

It had something to do with her passion for going out drinking with the girls every night, but I didn't know what to think about it.

I too, had a problem with alcohol in the past, and it was just another thing we had in common. I could save her. She seemed to think so, too.

Finally, a contrast between the two of us struck me -- I was strictly vegetarian, and Cat ordered rib eye steak, and a hot Fudge Sunday. She wanted no vegetables on the side, and told the waiter to take them away. I wondered, could a change in diet help fight the craving for alcohol? If only I could introduce Cat to a vegetarian diet.

The first mistake by me was thinking I could change anything at all about her, even for her own good. The issue of diet would be the substance of many an argument we would have in the future. She adamantly refused to eat any fruits or vegetables at all, ever. If she had her way, her diet would consist of nothing more than steak and chocolates. This problem hadn't blown up yet, and I was speculating on how we would come together on everything. It was a miracle that fate had brought us together… so wonderful. Chocolate is wonderful, too.

"Hey, well, so are you planning on going out drinking tonight?" I asked.

"Well, yeah, probably." She said.

"Why can't you go out with me? I'll take you to a bar or something, I don't know. I never go to bars, but I'm sure you know some places, and you can show me something."

"I like to go to a bar with a pool table. You play pool?" she asked.

"Yeah, sure, I know how to play pool."

"That would be fun," she said. She seemed excited, and I was certainly thrilled at any plan involving being with her. I wondered what we might do for the rest of the afternoon… assuming we'd go to the bar in the evening. But Cat was ready to play pool as soon as we left the restaurant.

She directed me to a bar that seemed a bit isolated, being in what had been an industrial area that didn't have any industry going on any more.

I watched her as she walked into the bar in front of me -- flinging open the double door. The bar had elegant antique wood paneling that had needed a new coat of varnish for some time.

Only three patrons were seated at the bar. It looked as if, at one time or another, a rugged bar crowd had frequented this place -- it didn't look like a place for a little girl. She was such a sweet girl, so petite and innocent.

At the moment it didn't matter what kind of crowd would frequent the place, because we practically had the place to ourselves. There was an available pool table -- as if waiting just for us. She went straight to the pool table, and in line with her businesslike demeanor -- aggressively racked the balls and started to chalk her stick like a pool shark.

"You break," she said.

I broke the balls, and none dropped in a pocket. She took her shot with one hand, breaking the balls further, and still none dropped. I made the 9 ball, then missed a rail shot. Cat sat on the billiard table, and with the cue stick behind her back, slammed the 2 ball into the corner pocket.

"Wow, you're good." I said.

She looked up at me, and without saying a word proceeded to clear the table -- one ball after another, sometimes with fancy tricks.

"I'm ready for a drink," she said, as the 8 ball slid into the side pocket.

We sat at the bar near a TV that was blaring, nobody watching, but it added to the atmosphere of the bar -- as if something was going on. The bartender came over, and Cat ordered a Rusty Nail. I ordered the same, coincidentally, one of my favorite drinks. I sipped mine, but she drank hers before I had taken a few sips.

"Are you going to order another drink?" She asked.

"Another drink?" I asked, barely having started mine...

"Sure, what would you like?"

She said that she wanted a Whiskey Sour, another of my favorites back in and day when I drank much.

"Yeah, I used to like that too," I started to say, as Cat waved to the bartender…

"Two whiskey sours, please," ordered Cat.

"OK," I said quietly, feeling awkward about having drinks stacked in front of me.

The bartender was talking to another patron—not immediately serving us.

Cat looked at my drink.

"You're not even drinking that. He might take awhile, and you're getting another drink, so let me finish yours."

"Sure, go ahead," I said.

She slammed down the Rusty Nail, and had her next drink in her hand before the bartender even set mine in front of me. Then we had several rounds of Whiskey Sours, with Cat finishing hers, and half of mine on each round. I was getting a buzz, but three times as much drink didn't seem to faze her. As much as I imagined we had in common, I had no ambition for playing pool or going out drinking with her. She could do that with the girls. Just then, one of her girlfriends walked into the bar…

"Ay Cat, how about some pool?" the girl said.

Cat nodded her head.

I looked at Cat. "I guess you won both contests with me," I said, and put a key to my house on the bar. "I'll meet you at home."

A couple of hours later she showed up at the house. "What a Pussy," she said to me.

"Well, I'm not a drinker or a pool player."

"She laughed, and said; "I know what you are."

We started kissing, and for the rest of the evening there was little talk.

At the beginning of my shift the next day I dropped Cat off at the place she had been staying -- with the one-eyed old man she claimed to hate. She was going to pack all of her stuff -- I'd pick her up later.

From then on, every night she went out with her girlfriends at night while I was at work -- then I'd pick her up and bring her home with me at the end of my shift. The few times I couldn't find her she was already at the house when I got there. For a couple of weeks she was with me all the time except for when I went to work, and even then she got me to take *love breaks* in the middle my shift.

Then one night she wasn't there -- not anywhere. I searched for her during my shift-- she wasn't around when I got home, and she didn't call. I was worried. My next shift would start with an anxious search for Cat. Then, just 20 minutes into my shift, the dispatcher called me; "79, you have a personal."

I snatched up the mic; "Yes… 79."

"79, Caitlin wants you -- California and Lindsay."

I was relieved, and glad to be just a few blocks away. I sped over to California and Lindsay, and saw Cat standing in front of a building near the corner.

She jumped in the cab, and had some news:

"I told my mother I was staying with you, and she said; 'I'm not having you shacking up with a man when you're not married,' that's what she said."

"What?"

"Yeah, and she rented me an apartment."

"She didn't rent you an apartment when you were staying with that one-eyed pervert—or when you were homeless."

"I know, it doesn't make sense, but my mother is very demanding, and when she found out I was with someone I really care about, she said; No, not if you're not married."

"So we have to get married to be together?"

"That would work," she laughed. "That's the only way to make it work. Don't worry it's no big deal, I just got an apartment here, and it's convenient to be downtown, but you can come over, or I'll be at your house anyway. We will work this out," she said with assurance.

"OK," I said, disappointed, and confused.

"Come on, let me show you where she put me."

We walked up three flights of stairs in a rundown building.

"Why this place?"

"My mother is cheap, she picked the place, and expects me to live here."

"You like it here?"

"I can't go against my mother."

"This doesn't make sense."

"Don't trip, she paid the rent already, and you can come over whenever you want."

I didn't like it, but I had a new pit stop at work, and started the shift every night going over to see Cat.

Women seek men for adventure, and men seek women for comfort. Cat's place suddenly had a party going on downtown, and plenty of adventure. I was beginning to feel very uncomfortable.

For a few days she still spent a lot of time at my house, but this diminished as her downtown acquaintances converged on her new apartment to party. There were also people who lived in the building; like the guy next door named David, who seemed to be flirting with Cat too much.

My relationship with a very special girl appeared to be in jeopardy. So, I posted at Cat's apartment to guard my interests.

Amongst Cat's acquaintances I met a lot of people that I didn't want to know. There was one woman named Frankie. She had a sneer on her face in place of a greeting whenever I saw her. She had a single tooth in front of her mouth. Her decrepit appearance suggested too much drug abuse, and I didn't like her at all. I called her *The Wicked Witch*.

Cat indicated having some kind of relationship with her. She was her girlfriend? A lover? I asked Frankie, and her emphatic response was that Cat was an idiot. She described how she would rip off Cat, and push her around. "She's stupid," said Frankie repeatedly.

I suspected that Cat's attraction to Frankie was based on the longing for the drunken mother who pushed her away. Frankie seemed to confirm this, saying; "She wants to be abused because of her need for Mama -- that's her problem." Whatever relationship Cat had with Frankie required a bit of imagination, because Frankie didn't seem to be a friend to Cat at all. Cat's world was crazy.

I observed madness in every corner at Cat's apartment. I tried to be patient with it as not to offend her. I couldn't figure out why this was happening. Then one day, as I sat in Cat's apartment alone with her, a new dimension in her life was revealed...

Cat asked me to sit in a love seat by her, and handed me a beer. I started to drink just to get along. I didn't really like to drink, and wanted to talk to Cat about her drinking problem. She'd been to jail for drinking several times, and was still going to court.

"Maybe it's time to quit," I suggested.

"I know, and you can help." she said.

Then, to my surprise, she pulled out a spoon, ripped a piece of cotton out of a cigarette butt, placed it in the spoon, and then set the spoon on a coffee table in front of us. She explained as she proceeded to put a little water in the spoon, and open a very small package of black tar...

"I met this girl in jail, and she was so cool. She watched my back, and that was important, because I'm small, and the other girls would beat me up. She was also a lot of fun to be around. When I got out of jail I saw the girl on the streets, and she invited me to go to a party with her. We had got pretty close, and she wanted me to try something new, and I felt obligated," said Cat, as she held a match under the spoon until the tar bubbled. "So this girl got me to smoke some crack, and try some heroin, and we had such a good time. The next day she was so friendly, and how could I resist getting high with her again. She got me high every day, on heroin, and then after a week she disappeared for a day, and I got sick -- real sick. She got me addicted. She showed up with a black guy in a Cadillac, and they gave me some dope so I could get well, and then they drove me over to Wilson Way and said; "OK, bitch, now get out there and make me some money."

"When did this happen?

"About six months ago," said Cat, as she drew the dark liquid into the syringe.

"You've been a heroin addict for six months?"

"About that, and I need your help."

"Of course," I said.

"Here, hold my arm." Cat said, as she positioned the rig over a vein to inject.

I was horrified.

"Come on, like this…or I could put a tourniquet on. You aren't much help."

I grabbed her arm as she had instructed, and she drew blood into the needle—registering a hit in the vein.

I was not as repulsed as might be expected, because at the very moment that these facts were revealed -- I was also told that she wanted to quit. So, instead of running away, the knot was tightened by a call to help my soul mate.

Later, I saw Frankie again. Of course they did dope together. A pathetic facsimile of a friendship they had -- to get high together so that one might not even know who they are. I confronted Frankie about it. Frankie laughed; "I'd do the dope and just leave the stupid bitch a wet cotton." I was under the impression that Cat even paid for the dope. "She's pathetic," Frankie said as she walked away. I was on a quest to figure out why such a problem could exist, and how to do away with it so Cat and I could have a life together. Frankie certainly would be no help.

I needed to talk with Cat about the drug problem, but when I went back to her apartment my attention was diverted by another problem -- Cat wasn't there. I wandered around the hallway for a while to wait, and then discovered that she was in David's apartment. She may have heard me pacing, and opened the door to see me in the hall. She ran out and grabbed me, and quickly took me into her place -- instructing me to be quiet.

"Why are you in David's?" I asked.

"Oh, he's an ass hole. I don't even like going over there, but he tricked me into coming in for a minute." she said.

"He tricked you?"

"He said he wanted to tell me something about you. I went over there and he told me that you're no good, and I shouldn't let you come around."

"Why would he say that? I think maybe I should knock him out."

"No, leave him alone. Don't worry, he's just a fool, and he won't get anywhere with me. I'm yours."

I lit a cigarette and kept quiet. Fighting this one guy wouldn't make a difference anyway -- the problem was the apartment. Her friends had the drugs and the alcohol, and we weren't going to solve any problems around this apartment. I had to get Cat back over to my house, and keep these other people away. I complained to Cat, and talked to her about the connection between the people and the drugs.

"I'll quit, and we can have a life together, but I'm just not ready yet," she said.

I wondered just what makes not ready? I had to get Cat away from the wicked women, and David -- as well as suspected other guys, including a supposedly rich man who wanted to marry her.

This woman, who seemed perfect in every way, turned out to have more of a problem than I imagined. So, should I walk away from my perfect match -- instead of help her?

People who would lead her to total destruction surrounded her. For all my concern, Cat called me her *Knight in Shining Armor*, and encouraged me to persist with my wish to rescue her. Yet, some rich guy wanted to marry her? And mama wouldn't allow her to stay at my house if we aren't married! The people she was connected with were a serious issue. It looked like a variation of a shotgun wedding at hand. But with all that was going on -- What was it going to take to really change?

"OK," she said, in response to my protests, "but I can't change overnight. The best thing I can do is to be with you, I agree, but I've had a lot of problems recently, and right now isn't the time to quit. I just wanna get high."

"How soon do you think you'll be ready?" I asked.

"I want you to get high with me. ...Then you'll understand."

"I don't want to get high. I want to help you quit."

"If you won't get high with me, I'll get high with Frankie."

Frankie was trouble. I had to stick with Cat. If I could get her away from other people that would be a big step.

"OK, I'll have some drinks with you, and smoke a little weed, but not too much; and we've got to make a plan about how to deal with all of this. A plan has to be specific; with details, and time limits. Can we make a plan?"

"Sure, we can make it just me and you, and we can do anything we want."

I still didn't know how deep these other relationships floating around the scene might have been. She wanted it to be just the two of us – that sounded like progress.

That evening we did nothing to make a plan, but we had

a good time. She was fun to party with. When she did her fix, she wanted me to do heroin, too, but I refused. Drops fell off of her spoon into my drink -- as a joke – and she called me a pussy again.

"I'm a pussy? It seems that you like girls… Is that what you mean?"

"No, but I love you, and you're the first man I've loved."

She had told me stories of being raped by her father and his friends when they were drinking.

We talked about her dominant mother, drunk and failing to hold her.

It all made sense that she would fall into such a disconcerting lifestyle as she had.

The question was: Now that I found her in this trouble, how do we get out of it?

In order to quit, I gathered, we might acknowledge that there is an underlying problem that led to drug abuse in the first place.

Secondly, we needed to pay strict attention to the people we associate with.

And finally, it would be necessary to find something else to do. It was clear what not being ready to quit meant -- Cat had too much baggage from her childhood, there was no way she was going to quit while surrounded by the kind of people she knew, and; What else was there to do?

I stayed at Cat's for 5 days, and for the most part kept other people away; except for a couple of apparently necessary visitors who Cat had to see alone -- and asked me to walk around the block so she could take care of something. Despite this, I felt like I had some control over the situation, but always on the edge, and Cat made sure of that. Determined to stick with Cat I'd been neglecting to go to work.

I didn't understand why a person would want to drink to the point of not remembering if they had a good time or not. When we wake up with a black eye, or with vomit all over the place, or otherwise feeling terrible; I couldn't see any of that to be evidence of a good time. And of course it could get in the way of doing the things we're supposed to do. From all the drinking that I'd been doing, I felt lazy, sick, and really didn't want to go to work – even though I should.

"Oh, come on and take another day off," said Cat.

"Give me a hair off the dog that bit me. Maybe I'll stay."

"Oh, you've got a hangover? Take a shot of the strong stuff. That'll fix it." She had a bottle of 151 Rum.

"No, no, I don't drink Rum. It makes me sick to think of it -- I feel sick anyway."

She also had some Scotch, and I opted for that.

A hair off the dog, and I thought of a shot, but she brought me a large tumbler filled to the brim.

I drank a little, hoping it would ease the pain. I'd never had such a hangover as this... My gut was wrenching, and it felt like my eyes were trying to pop out of my head from a fight pounding inside. I was sweating profusely. I took another drink from the glass, and wondered how anyone would want to do this, as I sat there holding a glass of Scotch in my hand -- sick, feeling like I was about to shit my pants. "Damn, I'm sick!"

"Do some dope with me," she said; "You'll feel better."

"No!" I insisted, as I finished the glass. Cat poured me another. I started feeling the alcohol, but still didn't feel better. I felt like my body was about to be torn inside out. My vision blurred as my eyes seemed to want to push out of my head. I looked up at Cat who was hovering over me with a syringe in her hand.

"Don't worry, you'll feel better-- I'll take care of you."

"Sure," I said, not intending to agree with anything, but suddenly Cat was on my lap sticking a needle in my arm. Instantly I felt better, much better, even wonderful. She'd missed a little in the course of sticking me several times with the needle. I came to realize that those little drops that Cat playfully spilled off her spoon into my drink were bigger drops than I thought. There was no more need to slip drops of heroin in my drink. The next day it was straight needle.

I was at Cat's another five days, and continued missing work. Even though all my bills were paid, I took note that I only had two nickels in my pocket. Meanwhile, Cat seemed to be trying to turn me into a pincushion. Both of my arms were discolored; with a few small lumps from slight misses.

"That happens sometimes at first," Cat said.

"Well, I don't like it happening to me. I'd rather go back to the drops in a drink."

"Are you sure?"

"Keep that needle away from me!"

"OK," and she squirted the entire contents of the syringe into my drink.

Just then there was a knock at the door. It was a woman that said her name was Butch, and the name certainly fit her character. I had met her before when we had a beer together. On that previous occasion, she had smashed an empty beer can in her hand, threw it on the floor, and then pushed me-- but in a friendly way. It was just her style.

"Hey motherfucker, how's it going?" said Butch, as she walked into the apartment, came over to me, and socked me in the arm. "Fuck, shit, God damn, what the hell -- it's all good. Lets have a beer," and she socked me in the arm again. She kept talking about the way the guys did it -- And had shown me by swearing a lot, and socking me in the arm.

"Hey, Mr.," I said, "I don't know what the guys you know do, but guys I know don't sock me if they want to get along."

"OK, I'm sorry," she said, and slapped me on the back rather hard.

"We're going to get along, so let's shake." I said. I have a rather strong grip, and she was, perhaps, nudged toward reality a little – as if I'd crush her hand. But if it did -- reality would never quell her manliness obsession.

One of her everyday tough guy plays was doing strong-arm robberies. It didn't always work well because she had a black eye a week earlier, and she had her nose broken once. She didn't seem to be giving up.

Now that we were *guys just hanging out*, she mentioned that she knew I had a gun, and it was hard for girls to get a gun...

I suppose the handshake turned her back into a girl, and the girl was eager to get on with playing tough guy -- and do it right by bein' a girl with a gun.

"OK, I'll sell it to you for $200, but you aren't planning on shooting anyone, are you?"

"No, I'll just hit 'em over the head with it -- but I could learn to use it."

"No, you can't shoot it -- you don't get any bullets."

"Awww," she moaned.

"I thought you said you didn't want to shoot it?"
"Well, maybe target practice."
"No."
"OK, I won't shoot it. So, will you sell me the gun?"

I needed the money after wasting so much time at Cats. So, the girl got the gun. Later, she got a bullet somewhere, and fired the gun in her backyard. The gun blew up into pieces, but she wasn't injured. She complained, and I scolded her.

"You said you wouldn't shoot it, and I told you not to."

She gave up on the idea of guns, and maybe decided it was too dangerous robbing people. The other people might have a gun, or some guy could kick her ass. She could go to jail. Maybe she learned a lesson worth $200.

♠ *In lacking a proper partition, it is easy to get caught up in the messes of your cohorts* ♠

It was more than three weeks that I'd been doing dope with Cat everyday. She said she ran into Sheila, the girl that got her strung out in the beginning.

"Oh really," I said with surprise.

Sheila told me; "Get him strung out – he'll buy your dope for you."

I thought it strange for her to tell me this. Cat had been coming up with all the dope. I didn't buy any of it.

I wasn't making any money, but I took the cab out every night – because we might need a ride to get dope. Most of the time the cab was sitting in front of Cat's building -- seven days a week now. What little taxi business I did-- I tried to hustle people into out-of-town trips.

Why wouldn't anyone want to get out of Stockton?

I managed to get a couple more people to take a taxi ride to Reno instead of the bus, and felt like maybe I had something going – but often had trouble getting any money at all, beyond what was needed for dope.

In order to break even I'd cruise around downtown from time to time, because I had established a rapport with the Mexicans. A lot of them were doing things that were illegal – aside from being in the country illegally. A taxi driver that was favorable to them was quite valuable in their world.

Knowing that I was not the police, but someone who might be helpful -- and trying to learn Spanish-language, I got a lot of referrals. I pretended to know more Spanish language than I really did in order to try to get along, and I was willing to negotiate fares, which made them feel good.

One day I agreed to give a ride that seemed to me to be just a few blocks away, from what I understood, for five dollars -- no big deal. My Mexican friend had referred his three companions to my taxi, and they all seemed rather excited that my service was available to them. They handed me $5 as they got in. Then, three blocks away they started firing pistols out the window. I inadvertently had agreed to do a drive-by shooting. I tried to explain that they couldn't do things like that in the cab. I don't know if they understood, but the four of them got out and ran down the street firing their pistols at someone. I became famous -- suddenly *Setenta Nueve* was in big demand. Considering the circumstances I didn't mind leaving the taxi parked in front of Cat's house as much as possible.

The rent was due, and mama hadn't arrived to pay it. I became concerned about getting Cat out before her mother, 'Queenie', paid the rent again.

"Is getting married the only way to get you out of here?"

"My mama...," she started to say.

"I know, so, tonight we can go to Reno and get married, and then you can come home with me?"

"Yeah, then my mother wouldn't trip."

"You want to go to Reno?"

"Let's go," she said.

The occasion dispelled my distaste for going Greyhound that night. We took the horrible 2 1/2 hour bus ride to Reno. We went to the Chapel of Love to make the marriage vows, and found out that we couldn't do it because Cat left her ID back in Stockton. So, we went back to the bus station and made the round-trip back to Stockton in order to get her ID.

When we got back to Stockton -- José had broken into my house and was inside smoking crack. The bus was going to leave. We had no time to deal with the problem. Somehow we found time to get dope, however, and Cat cooked it up in the little bus restroom. Back in Reno we got married that night. I was about to have an unbelievable honeymoon. As soon as we got back to the hotel, marriage certificate in hand, Cat said; "I'll be right back."

"What?" I asked, surprised.

"On the way into town I saw money out there."

"You're going out for tricks?"

"Nobody knows me here. I can get some money, and we need the money. You haven't really been going to work," Cat said, as she walked out the door.

I sat in the room wishing I had some dope, or something, and wondered what I had fallen into.

Cat was back in about an hour with a pile of cash, and a

big bag of dope.

We had a honeymoon all right, but far from what I'd expected. I heard that everything changes when you get married, but I never would have imagined anything like this.

Cat called her mother; "Mama, I'm in Reno, and I just got married."

"Oh my God," said Cat's mother. I called my mother -- who had exactly the same response to the news. We didn't care to say any more about it and invited our mothers to talk to each other.

We sat down in the backseat of the bus, and headed back to Stockton.

"When we get back," said Cat, "I want to get some dope and go straight to the house."

"OK, what about the apartment?"

"I'll just give the key to Frankie."

"Give the key to Frankie?"

"Well, I'm not going to be staying there, and with two weeks left on the rent -- might as well let her have it."

"I would do away with Frankie."

"Never mind that, I'm with you, we're married now, and mama can't say anything. We can be together now."

"We need to clear up this business with your mama, too."

"Who's that guy at the house?" Cat said, changing the subject.

"José, he used to work around there as a handyman."

"He's kind of cute -- you sure he isn't your boyfriend?"

"Come on, Cat, don't say that."

"I'm just kidding, but what is he doing in our house. It's our house now that we're married, and I want to know what your boyfriend is doing in there."

"I don't have a boyfriend, José just broke into the place to smoke crack."

"Do you smoke crack with him?"

"I hate crack, and I want you to quit. You said if we got married we'd quit the dope together -- the heroin, and everything. You don't still want to smoke crack do you?"

"You're stressing me out with all these questions."

"We need to talk about quitting drugs," I said.

"I want to talk about José," she said.

"There's nothing to talk about. Let's not argue, let's not talk about anything right now." I bit her ear, and she punched me in the stomach, and then kissed my face. I grabbed her and held her close.

"Yes, hold me close," she said, and we cuddled the rest of the way back to Stockton without any more talk.

Married life requires certain responsibilities and compromises. Our marriage was to heroin, and everything revolved around the dope -- that was the responsibility, and there would be no compromise. Of course, we were supposed to quit together, and Cat insisted that we would quit, soon, but not yet. Everyday we left the house together, and I went to get the taxi while Cat went downtown to get the dope. We had settled the argument about Cat turning tricks to get the dope. She showed me some *Hooker Magic* over several days, until I was disgusted. It was an ability to simulate having sex, and very convincingly, without really performing the act. She was a real professional. It was pointless to argue, anyway.

"I'm not going to stay home and play 'Suzie Homemaker'," said Cat, "I'll go get the dope, and wait for you to pick me up."

Every night, within an hour or two into the shift I would find Cat somewhere downtown -- bag of heroin in her pocket.

Even if it took longer for me to pick her up --she didn't seem to mind, even if she was sick. She could wait, as long as she had the dope in her pocket.

Doing the dope with me had become part of her drug addiction ritual, and she had to wait for me. I had the spoon, and the rig, and eventually would control the dope.

I would hog the dope so that she would do less, and eventually I would get her to cut down that way.

She didn't even seem to notice -- the routine was more important than the substance. I was a significant part of the routine. That's what made our marriage work.

It was three weeks before Cats mother came to visit. I was anxious to meet her until the time came when I actually did. People called her *'Queenie'*, but I called her *'The Dragon Lady'*. When I opened the door slightly she shoved her way in, and almost knocked me down, spitting fire at me, marching into the house and opening drawers and cupboards, then turning to me; "It doesn't look like you're taking very good care of my daughter. You don't even have any peanut butter here."

I ignorantly fought back; "Your daughter is my wife, and I'll take care of her. She only associated with women, because she was afraid of men -- on account of being raped by her father and his friends when she was a child."

Queenie stopped cold. "What did you say?"

"She's got psychological problems from her childhood,

and it led to her becoming a drug addict and a prostitute, and I'm here to help her quit."

"Cat! Is this true?" demanded Queenie.

"Well, aah, yeah."

"I'll check into this. You'd better treat my daughter properly. I'll be back."

"OK, fine, come back anytime," I said.

Queenie's fourth husband, Earl, had come with her, but kept his distance and didn't say anything. Queenie left in a rage, and Cat, of course, was quite upset.

"You didn't have to tell all; and you don't know what my family's like – they're all shh, shhh, shhh," Cat said.

She definitely wanted to get high now. I had hogged the dope to the point of getting Cat to cut down to a little more than a dime a day. If I was making progress, it was over with-- suddenly Cat was about to jump back up to $40/day. I don't think Cat ever did the dope without me except for when her mother came around. This visit kicked it up ...after she disappeared on me for the rest of the day.

The following night it took a little longer to find her, but she wouldn't leave me sick, and when I did find her she had quite a lot of dope. We were supposed to quit together, but it wasn't going to happen -- not anytime soon.

Queenie came back a couple of weeks after I had made the declaration that sent their family into turmoil. Queenie & Earl both explained to me that they had investigated this situation thoroughly, and none of it happened -- Cat was a liar. I didn't know what to say, but Queenie did; "...And I'm not having you conducting psychotherapy experiments on my daughter. You aren't getting her off drugs; the State will get her off drugs. The State, not you, the State."

It was too much for me to think about, and I effectively gave up. I had fallen off the fence that I had walked precariously for so many years, and got myself caught up in one of the very things I despised.

Our lives were tightly woven together, but for whatever similarities we had – the perfect match was revised to something to fire up the spoon. Cat wanted to smoke crack too, and we added crack to the routine. I always hated cocaine, and nobody who knew me would've believed that I would ever become a heroin addict, either.

The routine was the same every day: Find cat downtown, go home and do the dope, smoke crack, have sex, take Cat back downtown. Then at the end of my shift -- find Cat again, and go home for more of the same routine. It was like an evil merry-go-round. Life became simple, especially simple when you can ignore paying PG&E, or other utilities. We burned candles for months.

Then one evening, at about 6:30, I hadn't found Cat yet. Instead of driving around looking, I decided to park at the most likely spot to find her -- by a grocery store at the corner of California & Weber. If I drove around I'd probably find her at that spot anyway, so I decided to just read the paper.

I grabbed a newspaper from the rack on the corner and got back into the cab. A large crowd of desperate looking people were jostling with each other down the block -- walking back and forth across the street, or doing something devious in the shadows, or waiting for something, arguing with someone, or just hanging out lost. I hadn't even opened the paper yet, and a guy approached the curbside window of my cab. He looked clean-cut. I rolled down the window.

"Are you available?" he asked. "I just got off work in the store," he said, to qualify himself.

"Sure," I said, motioning him to get into the back. I held up the paper as he got in with a sandwich. He could eat his sandwich while I read the paper. I was stalling to see if Cat showed up. He didn't seem to care, and we sat and talked, while I looked over the news.

"Those people down there might not be the real problem, but just a symptom." I said, glancing up from the paper, and looking down the street.

"Yeah, they've got a problem, and I walk home with a '45' so they don't dump their trouble on me," he said.

I looked up to check out the guy more carefully. "Where do you live?" I asked.

"On the other side of Mariani's," he said.

"You might need two '45's -- the police can't protect you," I commented.

"Oh, fuck the police. They'd get me for protecting myself; it doesn't make sense, but people go along with the *public safety* bullshit, and silence implies consent."

"You sound like some kind of lawyer now."

"No, I work in the store, but I had trouble before -- drinking, drugs, and trouble with the law. I got out of it -- clean and sober for three years now. Working in a store on a horrible corner like this reminds me about what side of the fence I want to be on."

"Yeah," I said, as I knew too well; "It's too easy to get caught up, and a lot of these people've got no hope."

"People will suffer as long as things are sufferable rather then risk the uncertainty of change."

"Didn't Thomas Jefferson say something like that?" I asked.

"Yes, in the Declaration of Independence."

"The situation didn't turn out like our founding fathers might've dreamed."

I held up the paper pointing at the headlines: *Missing Children in our Time*. "They might be right down the street."

"They're in trouble, and they can't get out." He said.

"Something is really wrong." I insisted, "People only get horribly caught up in the absence of attractive alternatives, and I know for sure that a lot of these people would like an alternative -- at least sometimes."

"And when that time arrives who can they turn to?" He asked. "They can turn themselves in and take their punishment."

"A lot of them have been to drug programs that failed," I added.

"It didn't fail for the people who run the programs to collect the money," he said; "And for insurance companies who decide what treatment to give."

"I think hanging out there would be punishment enough," I said, pointing down the street. "You want to go?" I asked, as I threw the paper on the seat.

"Of course, but I was enjoying just sitting here talking; and I feel lucky to get a cab," he said. He got out for a second to throw his sandwich wrapper in a garbage can.

"So where are we going?"

"Lincoln & Anderson."

"That's scary enough," I said jokingly.

"Not as scary as these people," he said; "People who might jump each other, and they jumped into relationships somewhere along the line -- now the kids are missing, and so are the parents. It's a vicious circle -- the kids grew up and went to prison, and it made them worse, and they're still missing right there down the street."

"At least parts of them might be missing," I suggested.

"Like part of their brain." He added.

As we rolled, the mob was thick for several blocks – a disturbing display of desperate people.

"There's no hope, nobody will help – just a lot of hate going on these days," he said, shaking his head.

"Who's in charge to blame for this shit?" I asked.

"I took charge of my life myself, because blaming someone else doesn't do any good -- even if it is their fault. I can't change them. It was hard enough for me to change myself." He expressed some useful insights; "To get results I have to deal with things within my reach. A fictitious person runs everything. How can I touch that?"

"Look at that," I said, pointing at the crowd; "If only people knew what they do. Those people didn't come up with that behavior all by themselves."

"Everyone's been showered with brainwash. I'd like to kick a fictitious persons ass," he said, sounding serious.

"Of course, sex and violence proliferate the airwaves on purpose." I said, in response to his claims; "Our ability to reason is compromised when our focus is fixed upon issues of survival. Images of violence tickle the trigger of fight or flight. Maybe a little adrenaline rush from a gruesome show on TV, but the natural animal instincts of fight or flight also shut down part of the brain -- so for that moment we are easier to manipulate."

"I never thought of that," he said; "The reason for violence on television is to make the advertising commands more effective."

"Anger, hate, and sex all cause changes in the balance of hormones, and brain activity in general," I emphasized; "Diminishing our consciousness." "They want us to be distracted by sex, or live in fear of each other -- confused."

"They want everybody to fight each other so we won't fight them," he said; "The real criminals are running the government through the TV."

"With the shows they orchestrate, they also come up with an excuse for justifying the need for more police," I added.

"A lot of sneaky tricks, and people believe anything when they are distanced from the facts. The government's just a boondoggle," he said.

"They certainly aren't trying to lift up society; just sell aspirin and hemorrhoid cream -- or fuck us in the ass till we need it."

"The whole world is a pain in the ass." He retorted.

"Individuals have no control," I said...

"People are too detached, and with the culture of Individuality practically annihilated... a weird caricature of Individuality is showcased in its place: greed, and selfishness...

The very thing that is needed is scandalized.

Individuality as a culture requires mutual support— encourages responsibility, and honor, and empowers individuals to actually do something for themselves, and for others around them."

"No, that's a thing of the past," he said, with a wave of his hand. "We're headed for slavery and they tell us it's freedom."

"Hey man, the self-destruct button is pushed."

The customer started laughing, "The self-destruct button is probably hooked up to the TV. We don't need gun-control we need more responsible mind control."

"That's not really funny, I got hit in the head with the bat; I think I'm better now, but these people who play with video games don't know what hit them, and there is no recovery."

"No, not really," he replied; "The jokes on us, people should've got together a long time ago. You can't let the government do it -- and we forgot the price of liberty."

"What's that?" I asked.

"Eternal vigilance."

Just then, as if from the TV set they sprang, a group of children ran across the street firing guns. Another group of youths came right behind -- ducking behind cars, and firing back. I floored it, and made a quick right, fishtailing around the corner as the customer laid low in the backseat.

"Are they shooting at us?"

"No, but whoever they're shooting at, they usually miss their targets, so we'd better get out of the way."

"You've got that right, and you're a damn good driver."

"I've had a little practice."

Within a couple minutes we arrived at the customer's destination, and I watched him get safely inside.

I headed back to Cat's favorite corner, hoping that the gun battle was over. I passed several patrol cars, and the buildings seemed to dance to the strobe of the police lights. Cops were standing around looking official, but of course the kids were gone. People were doing drugs within shouting distance of the cops, and seemed to be enjoying the show.

It was a show that I was getting tired of being forced to watch. I'd been a heroin addict for nearly a year. It didn't change my character -- I didn't ever steal or sell drugs to support my habit. I could come up with excuses to justify a claim of good character -- embracing denial about the harms of being a drug addict. People who knew about my situation (other dope fiend's) would act as if they pulled my covers -- claiming that I was forcing Cat into prostitution to support my habit.

At some point everyone wants to quit this type of thing -- or any behavior that is harmful to themselves, or harmful to good social interaction, but, as is usually the case; the drug had become my social life. I played the game, but even still, I continued to find it unacceptable – I was sick of drugs, and the habits of other people who do them. Strangely trapped in a lifestyle I loathed …I wondered -- couldn't that apply to quite a lot of ordinary people too?

I made it back to the corner, and sure enough Cat was there. It was time to talk to her about quitting, but no, right now it was time for us to go to do the dope.

"Cat, are we ever going to quit this? The dope just makes you sick."

"No, stupid, not doing the dope makes you sick.

"Well, are we ever going to quit?"

"Are you sick right now?" She asked.

"Of course, and I'm tired of it."

"Well, I've got dope, so let's go get well, and we'll talk about quitting later. I'm sick and I don't want to argue "

"All right, Cat."

We went home and did what we always did.

The following day, after waiting awhile, I left the corner of California & Weber at about 6:30 p.m. -- Again, I didn't find Cat as early as usual. The search was on, and on the trek to cruise Mariani's no peculiarity would surprise me. The streets were dark, and the crowds on the streets were thinned – pulled back, and lurking in the shadows. A woman was lying motionless on the sidewalk in front of a large apartment building. When I got to Mariani's I didn't see Cat there, but I saw one of our other taxicabs -- cab number 86 -- cruising the area with a black woman driving (and the cab company didn't have a black woman driver). I dismissed my suspicion, and continued to cruise around looking for Cat.

Back on California Street I saw Jesus, a Mexican who had come north looking for work. Instead, he got caught up smoking crack, and living with a dope dealer. He was a nice guy that wanted out -- and feeling like a victim, he wanted to rip off the dope dealer and go back to Mexico. I had been talking with him for about a month. He got me to agree to give him a ride to the border for $1000. I didn't care how he got the money -- I had nothing to do with it, but I didn't mind helping him escape, either. He was a good guy in a bad situation.

I had to find Cat, but to make plans to give a ride to Mexico for $1000 was a compelling distraction.

I pulled into a parking lot to stop and to see how Jesus

was doing. As Jesus walked over to my car I looked around anxiously to see if Cat was in the area -- maybe Jesus was ready to go, and it would be an opportunity to get Cat out of town for a minute, too.

Jesus, standing at my window, didn't have a chance to say anything before some guy appeared out of nowhere, cocked a pump shotgun, and pointed it at Jesus' head.

I casually backed the cab out of the parking space and left the lot.

On the way back over to Mariani's, the woman was still lying on the sidewalk -- now with yellow police tape around the area -- she was dead. I saw cab #86 a couple of blocks down the road with a driver I was familiar with, and the black woman was now riding on the passenger side. I drove around Mariani's for a while -- not interested in driving back to California Street just yet. I gave a couple of rides to the South Side, and it was approaching eight o'clock before I decided I'd better race back over to California Street again -- Cat definitely wasn't around Mariani's. As I sped down the street I saw cab number 86 standing at a 45-degree angle -- crashed up a tree. The dead woman was still lying on the sidewalk. Cat still wasn't around California & Weber. I had to find Cat, but I had to take care of the taxi business, too, so I took a radio call for one of the downtown bars. It was one of the hookers that I knew fairly well, and she had some news...

"Ambrosia got stabbed 107 times and she still had the crack pipe in her hand, yeah, they found it right there -- it probably still had the coke rock in it." The woman rambled on with excited concern; "Somebody got her under the bridge. She was thinking she's gonna smoke a rock. They found her there with the crack pipe still in her hand."

It seemed, in a way -- the big deal about this brutal slaying was that she didn't get to take her crack hit. The woman wasn't helping my mood. I started feeling desperate during the half-hour it took to take this whore home and get back to looking for Cat.

Finally, at about 9:30 I saw Cat getting out of a car on Weber Street. I pulled up to Cat just as the car dropped her off and sped away. Cat jumped in my cab, and before I could get angry, she put me in check;

"I'm sorry, but look," Cat said, as she held out both of her hands. She had what looked like about a gram of the dope, as well as a handful of rock cocaine.

What could I say? I knew the routine. But I felt it was time to change the routine, and on the way to the house I told Cat about Ambrosia, and Jesus, and the taxi up the tree; and drove by the dead woman who was still lying on the sidewalk... surrounded by yellow police tape... no one in sight, no one to care.

"Cat, can't you just stay home?" I asked.

"We've got enough dope to last a few days if you hang onto it," admitted Cat. She handed me the ball of heroin, and the biggest rock -- about $75 worth of crack.

All that we had was enough to last us awhile, but it wasn't going to -- it was time to party. Of course, if she shared with some of her friends, then they would return the favor later -- and she wanted to do that. At least I got Cat to agree to stay home... as long as some of her friends could come over and smoke crack. She also agreed not to share any of the heroin.

When people smoke crack they often take a short piece of glass tubing, and shove a small piece of Brillo pad in the end. They melt the rock onto the Brillo, and then apply a flame to smoke it. Some people make a pipe out of a baby food jar -- by puncturing the lid with two holes, shoving a ball of Brillo pad into one, and a hollow tube (like a pen barrel) in the other hole for a mouthpiece. When using a jar, seeing the smoke swirling inside seemed to be a big part of the thrill of smoking crack.

I could think of so many absurd rituals throughout history that some people still like to believe – so the drug rituals didn't seem so odd.

What the smokers tend to do is take a hit, and then moments later want more. The high is a pleasant lift that only lasts for a few seconds, and then a craving rises.

If they get another hit right away they might not even get a lift out of it... and they don't even get high... just want more.

If they take a really big hit they might experience paranoia, and do something like peek out the window at nothing -- staring outside between the curtains.

Wanting more, crack fiends often search the carpet looking for any white crumb of something, and put it in their mouth to taste -- in order to see if it's got cocaine in it. They would search the carpet even if there was no evidence whatsoever that a rock had ever dropped on it.

Or, they scrape the pipe for any residue that might be in it -- even for hours after the last bit had been wiped out. A bizarre eight-person circus got kicked off at our house — all bad clowns, no audience.

A guy was peeking out the window, and you couldn't pull him away from it – frantically looking out at nothing. Two girls, and a guy were digging into the carpet on their hands and knees. Cat, and two other women were scraping their pipes.

I was doing some of this stuff too, and it irritated me. Perhaps I could see myself better than other people -- I don't know.

To be searching the carpet for the rock that was never dropped was really stupid. I caught myself doing that, and it really pissed me off. I kicked a cat box that was in the corner, scattering cat litter across the carpet. It didn't deter the desperate searchers, and a couple of the fiends started putting white pieces of cat litter in their mouth to test.

I watched the party, disgusted, feeling uncomfortable, and anxious for the drug to wear off. You'll always want more, but if you take another hit within a couple minutes it just makes you want more even more. I had taken a big hit, and just wanted it to wear off.

As I watched the fiends, I realized that if I wanted to get high on this stuff I had to let it wear off anyway-- or I'd just get caught up in a fiend routine.

Finally, I took a small hit, and got a little lift off of it, but not too much. Of course I wanted another hit, but I knew it would just make me fiend—not get me high.

Cat was busy scraping the pipe -- insisting that there was still a hit in it. Eventually, she would put another piece on, and pass little rocks around to her friends. They'd take a couple of hits in a row, and then get engaged on a mission.

It didn't look like any fun to me, and I decided that before I took another hit I would wait 20 minutes – I'd get a little high, but I didn't want the fiending—the craving was torture to me.

♠ *Control the drugs, or the drugs will control you...*
... unfortunately, drugs can put you out of control ♠

Cat ran out of rock, and then they all were scraping empty pipes for hours. I continued to take a small hit at 20-minute intervals. The high is really no big deal. I began to realize that without the engagement in senseless rituals, as if on an important mission, smoking crack was very boring.

Cat suddenly took note that I wasn't scraping my pipe, but I was periodically taking another hit.

"Hey, give me a hit," said Cat.

"You've got more rock?" asked one of her friends.

"Can I have a hit too?" asked another.

"Sure, I can give you all a couple of hits," I said, and set a large rock in the middle of the kitchen table.

They all were quickly seated around the table, and I broke off a small piece of the rock for each of them. They all took a hit, and by now could enjoy a little high for maybe 30 seconds. Within a couple minutes there was mewling about another hit.

"You agreed to wait 20 minutes before you got another hit," I said.

The group was either staring into space, or fussing with their pipes, and trying to act patient for a few more minutes. A hand started to creep towards the middle of the table where the rock sat. I raised a fork and stabbed the hand.

"Hey, that's fucked."

"It won't get you high. It'll just make you want more, and you've got to wait another 10 minutes."

The rest of the group was getting tired of my terms, and began to protest...

"Aw, come on, give me another hit."

"Yeah, how about just a small crumb?"

"Why do we have to wait?"

"Can I have a hit now, please?"

"You've got to wait a few more minutes," I told them all.

"You're fucked to party with," said one.

One of the girls got up; "I'm going out to make some money, and get my own rock. I'll get some dope too, and come back and get you well, Cat."

"Your husband is an ass hole," said another girl -- as she left, leaving the door wide open.

"I'm outta here," said one of the guys.

Momentarily, I was sitting at the table alone with Cat -- who was staring intensely at the rock.

"OK, go for it," I said.

Cat quickly snatched the rock and placed it on her jar.

"Cat, can't we quit the crack?" I asked with frustraion.

"I understand," said Cat; "And after this we'll quit the crack. We haven't been doing that much dope every day, so I'll just stay home -- but you gotta make sure I got some dope every day."

"No problem!" I said, "If we're not smoking crack, and just doing dope, and not doing much, we can try to quit."

"OK," said cat.

Cat stayed home, and I came up with a dime of dope for each of us every day. It seemed like it was working, but I suspected she had people coming over to the house when I was off at work. She seemed to be too concerned that I might be cheating on her. I took it as an admission of guilt. She was cheating. I wasn't cheating. But she was sure I was cheating, because I wasn't looking for her out on the streets, and I certainly was talking to other girls. Then I told her I had a run in with *Lady G*... So, I did talk to some girls, but so what?

"I know Lady G.," said Cat. I wasn't surprised that she knew her. "You'd better watch out for her," said Cat.
"You're telling me?" I said.
I had nothing to hide, and Cat knew better than to worry about Lady G and me, but I didn't want to tell her what had happened...

Earlier that evening...

I had gone into a grocery store to get a cup of coffee, and when I came out Lady G. was sitting in the front seat of my taxicab. She sat silently, and angled me with her Asian eye as I jumped back into the driver's seat.
"Hey, I have to go back to the Company for a couple of minutes," I told her.
"Alright," she said.
She didn't seem to need to go anywhere, and perhaps just wanted to go along for the ride. She was an attractive girl, and had been pleasant enough, and entertaining in the past -- demanding sex with her graphic suggestions.
"What?" I asked, "You just want to go along for the ride to get out of downtown for a few minutes?"

"Yes, fool, you know what's up," she said slyly. She continued talking, rambling on as I drove off — acting as if we were to enjoin in some sort of sinister romantic plot.

"I just have to go to the taxi lot real quick, and then I'll drop you off back downtown."

"Is there a bathroom there?" She asked.

"Yes, you use the bathroom while I drop something off to the dispatcher."

I pulled into the taxi lot, and as I got out to go see the dispatcher I directed Lady G. to the restroom. Lady G. lagged behind in the cab for a moment. When I returned to the taxicab she was still in the ladies room.

I noticed the gleaming of metal on the floorboard. I reached down to find a highly polished, razor-sharp, survival knife tucked under the passenger seat. I put it back as I noticed Lady G. returning from her call to the ladies room. She got back into the cab, and sat down as if poised for action.

She looked at me strangely for a moment, then as if the female spirit in Gaelic lore -- said to presage death -- had just landed on my cab, she let out an ear piercing shrill howl. Then made her demands:

"You took $167 from me, give it back," she said. She was reaching under the seat. I prepared myself.

"I've got you now -- you ripped me off," she screamed.

"Hey," I replied, "I didn't take anything, and you know that."

"You ripped me off! Give me the money," she said.

"What are you talking about? I'm not giving you nothin'."

She lunged at me with the knife in hand, and I flung open the door -- jumping out simultaneously with the thrust of the blade. My jacket was barely penetrated by the incredibly sharp point. She jumped out of the car after me. This woman was serious!

Thinking that this mad Amazon would surely cut me to ribbons,

I ran to the office--Lady G. right on my heels in attack mode. I slipped inside, and held the door closed with my foot as I tried to find the lock.

Lady G. was banging wildly on the door with the butt of the survival knife, yelling; "Give me $185. Now!"

I held the door shut with my entire weight as I continued to try to lock it.

Alice, the dispatcher, looked up as if out of a slumber, and matter-of-factly said; "Hey! Stop that. Don't be doing this kind of shit around here."

"Yeah, right Alice… one of these days… I mean, that really is astute advice," I said sarcastically.

Cat didn't really need to hear the story, and I didn't tell her – but she could imagine, and she wasn't about to miss the excitement on the streets anymore.

"I'm not staying home while you're out there fooling around," she said. She was putting on her coat and heading for the door.

For the next few weeks -- I would get the dope, or Cat would get the dope, or we'd both get dope. Within a short time we got back up to $40 a day. Even only 40 would become hard to bear as our habits surged to new heights. We maintained the well-established routine of always doing dope together -- Cat really liked to go to our house to get high.

We agreed not to argue, but write down our complaints in a book, and write back to each other—rather than get in shouting matches, and it worked.

We were getting along quite well, but falling far astray from the right direction. We had recently been talking about quitting, but now we were increasingly doing more dope. Cat was also back on crack.

"Cat, we've been having a good time lately, but what's it going to be, because…?"

"I'm sick," said Cat, "Wait 'till we get to the house."

"I'm tired of this. Why do you have to smoke crack, too?"

"You're stressing me," said Cat, "I just want to take a hit as soon as we get to the house. Maybe you could cook the dope for me while I take a hit."

"Why do you have to smoke crack before you do the dope? I'm sick of this, Cat."

"Let's not argue – just cook the dope," Cat said.

Thick smoke swirled in Cat's jar while I danced a spoon over a candle flame. This was our romance, but after Cat sucked the smoke out of the jar it did something to her -- it made it hard for her to find a vein. I filled my outfit with the dark liquid, and just squirted it on my tongue. Cat kept stabbing her wrists -- not getting a register. Blood was dripping off her fingers onto the kitchen table. She finally got well, and then immediately wanted to take another hit off of her jar -- and then another -- until it was all gone.

"Cat, we've got to do something about this."

"I know," Cat said impatiently, her attention intensely focused on her crack jar. The rock was gone, but there was residue -- maybe.

"Cat, you need to set down the jar for 20 minutes. You're not getting high, you're not thinking, you're just stuck."

Cat fussed with the jar for 35 minutes, practically

ignoring me -- she refused to stop.

"Cat we've got to talk about this. We've got to make a plan."

Cat continued to fuss with her crack jar -- trying to get another hit out of it, scraping it with determination.

"Cat there's nothing in there. Just set it down for couple of minutes. You've been scraping that pipe for over half an hour." I grabbed the pipe out of her hand, and grabbed it so hard that the jar shattered under my grip. As the baby food jar exploded, Cat went into shock -- she started trembling, then screamed, running out the door, and stomping her feet into the road as she ran down the street, wailing in despair.

"There was a hit in there, too," she said, when she came back a few minutes later; "You wrecked everything!"

"Come on, Cat, we've got to talk about this problem."

"Right now I want a crack hit, and I'm going downtown," Cat said, as she walked away. Such was the nature of our lover's quarrels.

After a few weeks our complaint book was almost full, and I wasn't hanging around Cat very much anymore -- except for when we were doing drugs. We always did the drugs together – quite loyally.

Whatever other fantasies we shared about a good life had faded.

She'd come home with me at night, but then sneak out again after I fell asleep.

I used to chase after her, but gave up after one morning when I found her on the corner covered with blood, and she described killing a rapist with a knife -- a very dramatic, detailed description.

Then, other people told me that she had been telling everyone that I was her brother, and that her husband beat her up all the time. Standing on the corner splattered with blood was just a scam to get sympathy -- and the brother talk didn't suit me well either. The whole scene left me so mentally fatigued that somehow I lost my ability to talk -- except in rhymes. Thus, was my last entry in the complaint book:

'Pleasures tossed and caught and lent, to weary mind so often bent...
Too wild a ride; now got to hide...
Who cares about some goddamn pride?
A gruesome trail... stuck in the mud, as steel mosquitoes suck our blood...'

With echoes of once a dope fiend always a dope fiend shamefully passing through my mind, the routine continued as usual for a couple of months -- I'd meet Cat between 6 and 7 in the evening, and then again later, between 3 and 4 A.M. ... We did about the same thing every day.

Finally, I got Cat to agree to cut down again, and I was naively hopeful we'd make it happen. We were doing less dope together, and I had to trust that she wasn't doing it without me. I was trying to wait a little longer before doing any, it was hard, and I had to wonder if Cat could handle it.
Could she just wait?

I was waiting, and getting sicker. Breaking out in a sweat, and feeling like I might shit my pants -- while every pain I had ever experienced in my life was re-creating itself. The time I scraped my knee when I fell off my bicycle at six years old -- my knee hurt now. Every pain I'd ever felt -- I could suddenly feel again, and more. The discomfort accelerated in waves. A hand was grabbing my guts and twisting, and I was being punched in the eye from the inside of my head. These were the withdrawal symptoms.

I wondered how much all this could be in my mind, and how powerful the mind could be.

Still waiting... my thoughts were interrupted by a broadcast from the imagination centers of my brain -- a lucid dream appeared, and an exquisitely dressed little man with a top hat & cane announced an extraordinary circus event;

"The greatest show on Earth," he declared, as the elegantly dressed little wizard changed colors.

Glitter would fly into the air, as he waved his magic cane and continued his announcements with glorious enthusiasm... "Step right up," he said, tapping his magic cane on the corner of California & Weber Streets -- the main place in town to get some good dope right now. Engaged in the cartoon going on within my mind, I became a rocketship flying to the vision of California & Weber Street.

"No way," I said to myself, snapping out of the intense daydream. "If I could just control my mind, how much of the addiction could I control?"

It has been said; the test for controlling your mind is to see if you can stop your thoughts. If you can't stop your thoughts, then how can you say that you can control your mind?

If I could stop my thoughts -- how might that help me stop addiction?

I had noticed how much the engagement in rituals and routine played a part in maintaining addictions. Automatic thoughts, rooted in our subconscious mind, are the most powerful driving factors of addictions.

Social systems, especially when they are dysfunctional, promote excessive automatic thinking. So… Advertising and other influences have inadvertently created a culture that is growing against free thinking.
Proliferation of popular addictions are promoted in normal everyday life… Caffeine, Sugar, Cigarettes, & more.
Properly adjusted people within the New World Order would get used to abuse, and perhaps, willingly spend their whole life slaving for a tyrant. A corral would be built to hold the subdued masses. Addictions aid this effort.
Corporations, and governments had become monstrous tyrants. There seemed no way out, because even the pillars of society had become no better than dope fiends -- stuck on stupid. They would levy exorbitant fines -- demanding payment from the poor. Build prisons that make criminals even worse. Have police crackdowns on honest citizens. Promote school systems that cannot teach. Yet, insist that everything is going fine.

Society would carry on, moving forward in a world of lies, as though an urn of hateful melancholy bubbles. Overflowing with wastefulness, and false-functioning foundations -- it is sure to enter chaos if the pundits of dysfunction don't resign. Why doesn't the prosecutor quit? Why doesn't the corrupt Mayor quit?

Wondering whatever frightening engagement was going on in their minds made me want to do drugs even more. I tried to resist the whirlwind of thoughts – which made it harder to bear the pain of withdrawal.

I wondered about the claim that some people can bear dental procedures while under hypnosis. I also wondered about the relationship between hypnosis, automatic thinking, silencing the mind, and the affects of the subconscious.

"What is this that comes out of my mind?" I asked myself, frustrated... "This is ridiculous."

Suddenly, I realized that I knew a trick to set myself free.

I can't ever explain it, but can try to describe it: I took a deep breath to the count of 10, expanding my gut as I inhaled. I let out the breath with a sigh, and tried to clear my mind in the process -- as if expelling the bullshit. I relaxed my toes. Focusing upon breathing and relaxing, and letting go of all else, I continued... Relaxing my knees as I let out a breath with a sigh, slowly to the count of 10. I repeated the breathing process, systematically relaxing my body. When I let out the breath to relax my torso, it was as if to expel all the programming in my mind with the wind -- releasing the paradigms and constructs that made up my subconscious, and the automatic thinking that sprang from this underworld within me. I'd blow away these thoughts, and declared it was my time to relax. I would think of nothing but breathing and relaxing. Abandoning all desire, I would cling to nothing.

Indifference was my doorway to salvation.

I continued to exercise -- breathing and relaxing. My mind became so still that I only acknowledged actuality in present time. By keeping my mind still for an extended time, I entered a perception untainted by labels or values. By letting go completely, I was able to dismantle all of the conditioning I'd ever been exposed to. Real *Willpower*, it seemed, was nothing more than the suspension of programming. With this insight, I was determined to stop my mind from wandering, and to try to purge the content of my subconscious -- I sat, totally relaxed, free of desire, intensely aware, not reacting -- unmoved by my environment. I dug deeper into a serene nothingness that was unfolding. Layers of programming stripped away as if I was reaching for the essence of my being.

Suddenly, I was overwhelmed by a feeling -- as if the gates of heaven were opening. A Perfect Universe appeared to be at hand. To touch the essence for the smallest fraction of a second -- Everything becomes perfect. Suddenly, instantly, I was released from heroin addiction. The withdrawal symptoms went away, **and did not return** ... believe it or not ... I quit cold with no withdrawal. What I really did to accomplish this is impossible to describe. If there was a way to develop a method of teaching this, we have, ironically, a society that is against it in a variety of ways. I had a way to quit, cold. I did it, and the way might be too confusing for the masses, but I had to figure a way to explain the method to Cat.

I wondered if this inexplicable mental trick I used might be related to hypnosis. I managed to find a self-hypnosis tape that was specifically designed to help people stop using drugs. On one side of the tape was guided imagery, and relaxation techniques -- similar to part of the process I used. On the other side of the tape was a subliminal message -- carried behind the sound of ocean waves and monotonous piano music. It was worth a try, but would Cat participate?

I had quit using drugs completely. Cat still said she wasn't ready. After a few days, some people were acting as if I had an attitude -- as if I thought I was better than everyone else because I quit.

A wide range of rumors attempted to discredit my success. Cat became emphatic about not quitting.

Subliminal persuasion supposedly doesn't work, but it seemed that it would be the only thing that would work against the resistance I was getting, so I wanted to try the subliminal side of the tape.

I drove around downtown looking for Cat -- I would tell her that I was working on a project for a music class at school. I had started going to school, because it's necessary to find something else to do when you quit drugs. I would tell Cat that I had to listen to this peculiar music to analyze it. I found Cat hanging out with three other girls by some bushes in the cuts off of Main Street. I parked the cab and walked over to them...

"Hey Cat, why don't you come to the house."

"I'm doing something," Cat said.

"Can you at least hang at the house for a few days -- at least it will be safer."

"If my friends can hang out there too, and you don't preach to us about quitting drugs – then sure, we'll hang out at the house all of the time."

"What friends?"

"I've got friends, and right now I'm trying to help Charlotte."

Charlotte was shivering wildly – had a bad hit from a dirty needle, or something.

"Taxi driver, it's cold, and I'm shivering to pieces," said Charlotte.

The other girls weren't helping – other than keeping her company.

"I know I'm just a piece of trash," said Charlotte; "Can you give me a trash bag, so I can crawl into it and keep warm."

"Cat, when are you going to come to the house?"

"I'm not gonna quit—not right now." she replied.

"Can we talk about it?" I asked.

"We're not gonna quit using drugs," said her friend Corey.

"Charlotte needs a trash bag," said Cat.

"Just dope, no crack at the house?" I asked

"All I need is a trash bag, please, I'll crawl into it," said Charlotte.

I looked in a nearby garbage can. There was a trash bag full of grass. I dumped it out and gave the trash bag to Charlotte.

"Yeah," said Becky, "Let's go, Cat, we can do dope over

there and relax—it's better than this shit behind the bushes."

"My dream is to smoke crack behind the bushes with my husband," said Cat.

"Come on!" I declared.

"To heck with the crack," said Becky, "Let's just get more dope and go to your place."

"You won't bother us?" Cat asked.

"No, I just have to play some music over and over to try to analyze it for a school project."

"That's cool," said Corey.

"So, are we all going?" asked Becky

"All right," I said, "Charlotte, get out of the trash bag."

All four girls came to the house, and all but Charlotte emphasized that they were not going to quit drugs. Charlotte only said that it was nice for me to let them use the house to get high.

Things had been getting rough on the streets, and Becky really liked the idea of coming to the house to do dope. Cat had always liked it. The girls ended up coming to the house all the time to do heroin, and continued to tell me that they were not going to quit -- knowing I had that in mind. I wasn't going to do dope anymore myself – even sitting around watching them didn't tempt me. We listened to the subliminal tape continuously.

"How come you keep playing the tape?"

"I've gotta keep playing it. I'm trying to memorize some parts for a project at school."

"He's going to community college now, and has a music class," announced Cat.

"That's good," said Charlotte

"I'm not doing drugs," I said. "It's something else to do."

The girls listened to the subliminal tape several hours a day for a couple of weeks. Suddenly, Cat was talking to me about seriously wanting to quit. I hadn't done any dope for 2 1/2 weeks. Cat was ready now. Becky was also talking about quitting. Cindy suddenly was considering.

I hadn't done anything -- just play the subliminal tape, so perhaps there is something to it. I told Cat what I'd been doing, and showed her the packaging for the tape. I explained that there's another side to it that will talk to her and help her to quit.

Her girlfriends had left, and it was time to go get some dope -- she needed to, she was sick. She agreed to try the tape instead, and the hypnosis tape successfully put her sleep.

The next morning she was craving the tape. She said that it works, and she told one of her friends about it.

She listened to the tape in the afternoon, and it put her to sleep again.

Her friend wanted the tape, so she could quit, too -- so her friend stole the tape.

Cat was very upset -- she hadn't done any dope for a day and a half, and she needed the tape. It only takes three days to kick, and we were halfway there, but I didn't know where to get another hypnosis tape. The other girl wasn't going to give it back. I had to think of something, and I decided to tell Cat a story... a story about climbing a rope. First, I got her to relax, breathing to my count of 10 – similar to the process of hypnosis, but not exactly. In a soothing tone, I told her a story:

...*Climbing the Rope*...

..."Now concentrate," I said, "Imagine that you're at the bottom of a deep pit. You see a figure there, an attractive figure surrounded by fun and games and sweet things. The light is dim, and there is a haze about the place, and a peculiar smell. You feel familiar with this place, but you're not really comfortable. You aren't satisfied, but you just can't seem to tell what is wrong." Cat sat quietly, relaxed, but began to fidget, and I continued; "I am here to help you. You are perfectly safe with me. You will feel comfortable, and for the first time you will be able to look behind the haze in this place where you've spent so much time." As I had her take another deep breath, Cat remained calm, and I invited her to imagine; "You smell the smell, and realize that it is actually quite unpleasant, but it cannot annoy you because I am here to comfort you." Cat fell deeper into her seat, as I instructed her to imagine that she was standing at the bottom of a pit. "Now look at the figure that commands the area -- look carefully now." Cat nodded slightly. "You can see through the haze, and you realize that the figure standing there is not an attractive person at all but the Master of Confusion. Look carefully, and see the figure is actually a lizard-like human form. It has a long red tail and puss oozing from the scales on its body. A long black skinny tongue comes out and twirls in the air, and you are amazed that you have been tricked into hanging out in this place with this beastly King of the Pit." Cat tensed, as I continued; "At the creatures webbed feet you see that the pit was not filled with fun and games, but with foolishness and wastefulness." ..."Old bones and trash lay about, and what you thought were candles were actually urns dispensing mildly poisonous gases. The stench is of stale tobacco and dope smoke, and this odor is growing increasingly unpleasant to you as you realize you had been tricked into accepting this place." Cat seemed to tremble a little, but appeared to remain calm. I went on; "Let go of it all now, because I'm here to help you escape. The power to distract you is weakened because I am here to help you, and you will be free of this place. You will no longer need anyone's help once you are completely free." Cat let out a deep breath, slowly, with a sigh. "You will, for the first time in your life -- truly be yourself, without fear." Cat appeared thoroughly relaxed at this point, and I proceeded with the story; "So, you look up now -- out of the pit. The pit is deep, and far, far up you see a beautiful crystal blue light, and once you see the light you notice the only attractive thing in the pit -- It is a rope -- a beautiful rope of gold and platinum threads. You grasp the rope and it feels good." Cats eyes remained closed the whole time, and she looked to be at peace. "Now, climb the rope," I said, with mild emphasis; "As you climb the rope you rise above the smoke and stench of the pit. You take a deep breath and enjoy the fresh air. The rope feels good between your fingers, and the exercise you get from climbing the rope makes you feel more alive." Cat was sinking into her seat, took another relaxing breath, and listened. "Down below, the wicked beast is calling to you -- offering new drugs and candy and beer and cigarettes." Cat stirred slightly. "You cannot be tricked by the beast -- the exercise, and the fresh, clean air has strengthened your mind." Cat seemed very calm with her eyes closed, as if sleeping, but I trusted she was hearing what I was saying.

"You can see it for what it is now. You can see its ugliness, and no longer will allow yourself to live in the life of illusion. You don't care to even look down the pit anymore. For a change, to feel really alive now, is good. As you climb the rope, you look up at the beautiful blue light you see at the opening. In the light your best friend from when you were a little girl is calling to you; and your favorite relatives are there calling for you -- anxious for you to reach the light. It is exciting, and you feel great joy. All of the mistakes you've made in your life -- you are leaving them behind. All of the pain you've experienced -- you'll leave it all in the pit. You struggle to climb the rope with joy. Up in the light is a lush paradise, and you look up and see famous people that you admire -- they're encouraging you, and you know you can make it because it's your life, and you want to enjoy it, and you will." I went on, with accelerating enthusiasm; "It is a long way up to the light still, and the beast is frantically calling from below, but you calmly ignore it -- nothing can disturb you now. The beast is calling from below, trying to trick you again -- insisting that you'll never make it. But you are your own true self now, and you will never accept failure again so easily. The beast is calling, yelling that you might as well give up and come back down, but you will never go down in the pit again. You'll enjoy your determination, and your persistence, and your positive attitude, and it all brings you pleasure because you know that nothing can drag you down anymore. Time and again, the beast is calling, and you are suffering to escape his clutches. The rope is getting difficult to climb, but the difficulty does not deter you. The demon is trying to trick you with enticements, and claims that you need drugs or cigarettes or unhealthy eating or other bad things in order to eliminate your discomfort, but you will not believe these lies anymore, because you know the discomfort is really just from the struggle of climbing the rope -- a worthwhile struggle. You are enjoying the exercise as you make progress towards paradise. You continue to climb the rope, and you are getting a pain in your gut from climbing so high, but when you look up at the beautiful light, you see your friends and relatives in the paradise above, and the pain does not bother you, because you know you'll be in paradise soon, and whatever the pain there is -- to climb the rope is worth it. Fresh fruits on the sides make you feel healthy, and give you more strength, and you continue to climb the rope, and you feel good. The beast calls to you, but you clear your mind and are unmoved by temptation. Even your favorite pet is up above in the light, encouraging you upward and onward up the rope. Despite the discomfort you are very happy, because you know you will make it, and the discomfort will be over with. You will continue climbing the rope up into the beautiful light in paradise, and everything you ever wanted will open up to you. You will enjoy it, and you will be proud of yourself -- you are your true self now in the dawn of your new life. As you continue to climb the rope you will be free, and it is all good."

♠

For the next couple of days Cat would visualize climbing the rope. She slept most of the time, but when she was awake she practiced the relaxation exercise, and continued to climb the rope. The process worked, and it appeared that we had finally escaped drug addiction. For nearly a week we didn't do any drugs at all, and I realized that we had to find something else to do very soon. Cat needed encouragement to hang on. I anticipated praise for our accomplishment, and was anxious to break the news to Queenie -- as she was due to come and visit.

When Queenie showed up, I assumed she would be proud -- She wasn't.

"We quit using drugs," I declared.

"You what?" asked Queenie.

"Me and Cat are both clean," I said.

"I told you that you're not going to do it... the State..., exclaimed Queenie.

"Cat, tell her," I said.

"Yes, mama, we quit," said Cat.

"Oh, bullshit," snarled Queenie.

Cat was becoming upset, and didn't want to comment anymore. Queenie wanted to go get something to eat, so we were off to a restaurant. At the restaurant, Queenie was caustic in her manner, but said little -- mostly incomplete sentences. She talked as if we weren't even there, and didn't matter. My attempts to get an acknowledgement were quickly rejected. Cat just sat and sulked in front of a grilled cheese sandwich that she didn't eat.

"Well, I guess we're done," announced Queenie, as she got up to escort us back to her car. "I'm tired, and I've got a long drive ahead, so I'll just drop you off downtown."

"No," I protested; "Our house is on the way."

"Look, I don't want to argue," said Queenie.

She had to drive by our house on the way to where she was going, but I wasn't going to tell her. Queenie became increasingly hostile, and I couldn't say anything more.

Cat was becoming quite upset as Queenie raced towards the center of downtown. I tried again to reason, but Queenie cut me off, simply saying, "No!" She abruptly pulled over the car at the corner of California and Weber, handed Cat a $10 bill, and said; "I'll just drop you off here."

"Why did she do that?" I asked Cat, as she stood on the corner with me -- in tears, trembling, with the $10 bill in her hand.

"The State, the State, the State – what does she think the State is supposed to do? I just want to get high now," said Cat.

"What are we going to do?" I asked.

Before she could answer, one of the dealers standing there on the corner -- familiar with what we always wanted -- snatched the $10, and put a dime of dope in Cats hand.

"Are we going to go back to doing dope again?" I asked.

"It was easy for you -- Maybe you weren't doing that much. I'm way too stressed-out right now, and I can't take it. I need to do some dope. Are you going to do it with me?"

She already had the dope in her hand, and I figured I could do some just so that she'd do less. "All right, Cat, let's go home."

To quit drugs, or any other bad habits -- having a goal and a plan, and seeking out some other engagement might not be enough. With drug abuse I noted that there was always an underlying problem that preceded the problem with drugs. We must resolve the foundation that our habits rest on, or change may be too difficult to bear.

Cat had an underlying problem that couldn't be overlooked, but looking at it was painful. The right thing may have become demonized in the face of cheating the wrong thing that we had grown so accustomed to.

I agreed to do dope with Cat, and I got strung out again – on purpose -- just so I could prove that I could quit, and maybe explain the process to others. Cat, upset by her mama, was most certainly about to be going on a binge. I was determined to stick with her.

"It'll just be for a little while, we know we can do it, but I'm just not ready right now," said Cat; "If we can get some money, maybe we can get away from here, and that'll make a difference. I'll go anywhere with you," she said, as she rubbed her cheek against my shoulder.

Within a few days we were back up to a $40 a day habit. We weren't going anywhere except on the well-worn path between the dope corner and the spoon. Cat wasn't going to quit. We started arguing a lot.

I went to see Val, and Frankie was leaving Val's house as I pulled up. I went inside, and Val was dying – her last words: "Don't give up."

What Frankie was doing at Val's, and questions about other suspicious things, enflamed my arguments with Cat.

Fights with Cat became an issue at my work, but the dispatchers had already been trying to get rid of me for quite some time, anyway. They often complained that I wouldn't follow instructions, and that I disappeared all of the time.

The owner, Thor, didn't want to tell the dispatchers that I was an independent contractor, and technically nobody could tell me what to do. The dispatchers wanted to feel like they were the boss, and they were up in arms about my belligerence. Thor confronted me, and explained that the turmoil was too much -- he had to cancel my contract. I had an escalating drug habit, the gas and electricity had been off at the house for months, and we had been riding on the edge of eviction -- Now I lost my job.

"Cat, do you think it's time to quit? We can't have a life this way."
"You don't have a job, and we need some money; so I'm going to get it, and you have nothing to say," said Cat.
Cat was too in love with the game of lies, and I was getting weary of it. I spent far too much time wandering around downtown in the middle of the night looking for her. We had to make a plan – and finally, Cat had a scheme in mind. While standing on the corner splattered with blood, she met a guy who wanted to marry her -- a very rich guy (I thought I heard something like this before).
"Just go along with me," Cat said; "I'll get some money, and then we'll get out of town together."
She was still telling me she wasn't ready to quit, but I'd had enough.

I quit cold using the same processes I had before: By becoming totally relaxed, clearing my mind -- not wanting, not labeling, and maintaining a clear, present-time awareness.

I got to a point that was something like a divine indifference -- At that point there would be an ecstatic rush, a feeling of timelessness, and for the briefest moment it was as if there was a reset button at hand.

I wish I could stop my thoughts and press that button any old time, but it's elusive, and not supported. The process is impossible to describe, because how can I describe a heightened awareness blended with total indifference? How can I explain wanting to want not? I wish I could tell you, but all I can say is that it worked... At the opportune moment I dismissed the drug addiction, without experiencing any withdrawals, and I would never revert to doing drugs again.

On the other hand, Cat wasn't about to quit -- Not yet, still. We argued, and she said; "The turning point of our relationship was when you broke my jar." She was smoking crack again too. She had to be high on drugs to pull off her schemes. "This guy is rich... just give me a couple of days," said Cat.

Later that evening, I watched my wife ride away with Chuck, the guy who wanted to marry her. That was the last time I ever saw Cat.

♠

A bowl of soup, a bed, a crust or bread, a place to wash -- the prospect of even a distant reward in mind may give life a semblance of purpose. A family to support, a girl to chase, an enemy to conquer-- these things keep us going even when there is no place to go to.

A bottle of wine, and a piece of tail from time to time makes up the best of some people's dreams. I mused, as I walked down the street looking for another unclaimed aluminum can -- just six more and I'd have enough for two potatoes and a beer. My feet hurt -- old shoes made in China, bloodstained from what the shoes were. I couldn't go far, but got a few more cans in line with my path to the recycling station -- a booth in the supermarket parking lot. I felt lucky to find two cans on the curb right outside the store. I had enough for an extra potato for dinner.

It was a good day, and the painful walk back to the house didn't bother me. I felt good, and enjoyed a slow walk by beautiful gardens and country pastures. It was Springtime, and a sea of yellow flowers lined the road. Walnut orchards were in bloom, and acres of tomatoes added a red color to the distant landscape. I wondered about many tomatoes lying on the ground. Farm workers didn't make much, but compared to scavanging for cans -- I had to figure.

The PG&E was still off at the house, and I was about to be foreclosed. I had somewhat readied myself to live in a field somewhere -- camping out on the side of the house.

The house was on a large lot, once with a spectacular garden, but not watered for over a year. I positioned myself on the lot with a campsite by a couple of flower bushes that had survived. I broke up sticks from dead bushes, and cooked a dinner of three potatoes on an open fire -- this had gone on for a few weeks. Confused, estranged from the world, alone, and trapped in a situation where 85 cents was a lot of money to me -- It was enough for dinner.

Unemployment was rising, and jobs were getting scarce. I would do farm work if I could, but I didn't know what to do.

Strange changes were taking place, and it was hard to figure where our nation was going. I had read in the paper that Bill Clinton had given favored nation status to China. What did that mean? In the same newspaper, on the same day, there was an article about a refrigerator factory in China that had been getting complaints. The government went in and rounded up all of the managers in the parking lot -- and had a firing squad. What did this all mean? Some global thing was going on, and I didn't know if I liked it.

Somehow a new thing called NAFTA was supposed to benefit us, but talking to neighbors who had small farms shed a new light. A guy named Doyle, who had a field of tomatoes down the road, told me; "I've got to get $10 for a crate of tomatoes, but all of a sudden they're getting shipped and delivered from Mexico for five dollars a crate."

This year's harvest would be the heads of many small independent farmers. Corporate farming was taking over, and soon numerous local food processing plants would also shut down. Everything was being outsourced, as if the country was being surrendered to an invisible enemy. Sustenance workers would be on the street fighting for cans.

Wal-Mart was coming into town, and there was a little protest, but Wal-Mart also seemed favorable because of their position of promoting American-made goods. Some people were optimistic that Wal-Mart would promote

American manufacturing, and manufacturing puts more money into the economy than anything else -- even people living in tents in tulle patches could get a job.

Nobody knew what would happen, but something was happening. I figured the country was being looted. Wal-Mart would prove to be a Trojan Horse. Maybe people would get beat down, and adjust, like I did, to a livelihood based on 85 cents a day.

The fire flickered in my face, as I shared my last potato with my dog. A local farmer had killed her mother -- a dog named after my wife. The puppy was anxious to be my only friend.

With questionable prospects developing everywhere, I was further burdened by being stuck in the middle of nowhere. How could I ever get a car on 85 cents a day? I remembered Val's last words, and upon that thought the fire flared up as if in approval.

I wondered if there was a reset button to fix a problem like this? I took a few deep breaths, and cleared my mind, focusing on a spot above and behind my head, as if waiting for a golden door to open from the heavens and shower me with riches. I snuggled up with my puppy by the campfire, and went to sleep, outside in the dirt.

In the morning I awakened to an amazing surprise. Family and friends from the Bay Area who hadn't seen me for a couple of years suddenly showed up. They knew I had a problem, and they knew that my wife was trouble -- but they didn't know any details. Since Cat could be blamed as a source of my problem, and she was gone, my family and friends suddenly volunteered to help me out.

To give me another chance to make it they bailed me out of foreclosure, and had the utilities turned back on. I was surprised to even hear from anyone. I got a break, and moved back into the house, but had less than a month to figure a way to get an income -- something better than what gathering cans could provide.

I needed to find a way to get a car, or I could be stuck on a corner with a cardboard sign.

Asking for something for nothing is not my policy, and I wasn't going to panhandle in front of convenience stores, or hold a cardboard sign at freeway on-ramps-- but I started asking total strangers if they'd give me a car.

That's as close as I ever got to holding a cardboard sign, because I knew -- if you take an easy way, like begging or stealing, you set yourself up to be stuck at zero. I was totally against the cardboard sign idea – even though some people claimed a windfall with it.

Both the giver and the receiver are wrong. You may feel good about giving a dollar to a person with a cardboard sign who has a well practiced pathetic look, but as you drive away feeling proud – they hate you for it – for looking down on them, playing into their lie, and actually ignoring their problems– paying them off so you don't really have to look.

Some of the beggars were taking in huge profits standing at freeway on-ramps, but I didn't want to get stuck there – I wanted to drive by them, and be glad I was not one of them. If I were going to ask for anything I'd ask for a car. Somehow I had to get a car, so I asked everyone. It wasn't working.

Pacing around in circles, wondering what to do, a knock

came at my door. I opened the door to Thor, smiling.

"How are you doing?" asked Thor.

"It could be better," I said, surprised to see Thor at my house. Then he asked:

"How would you like to buy my cab company?"

What a stupid question, I thought. "Yeah, sure," I said. He knew I didn't have any money.

"I'm going to sell it to you nothing down, and you just make the payments."

"Fine," I said, not believing what I was hearing.

Thor just stood there, smiling, without saying anything. 'Now what?' I asked myself, feeling awkward.

"I'll come over tomorrow morning, and take you to sign some papers," said Thor.

"I'll be here," I said, still not knowing what to think.

The following morning Thor came by and brought me to an office -- where I signed a sales contract, and a document transferring 40,000 shares of a corporation into my name. Then he drove me to the cab company and told people; "Meet your new boss."

Nobody else ever wanted to drive my old taxi, and it was still sitting on the lot. The crew looked at me with shock and awe as I grabbed the keys to number 79, and drove it home -- leaving Thor to explain things. The following day I was told that the head dispatcher had a nervous breakdown, and was going on permanent disability.

For the next few days Thor educated me about the various operations of the business. Most of the cars had too many miles on them. I'd have to get more cars soon.

"When going for inspections," said Thor, "change the backseat in the cab, and put one in there that has a spring sticking up through it. The inspector will be able to find something for you to change, and it's easy for you to change the seat. But if you don't do something like that, then they'll find something else, and I might not be so easy a fix."

I was sick of the wastefulness, and harms of distanced controls, but there was nothing I could do about it -- *Authorities* had grown too large. As a defense against bureaucracy, I had to agree with Thor about his inspection method. But there was more...

The vehicle identification numbers had been changed by the mechanic on almost all of the vehicles in order to avoid smog testing. I didn't like that.

Some, or all of the employees had to be paid under the table because of legal issues. I didn't like that.

Some of the employees were heavily involved in drugs. I didn't like that, either.

There had to be a catch to this blessing, so when I went to an auction to get a badly needed car I put it in my name instead of the name of the corporation--just in case.

After a few months I had a good enough income to pay off people who had helped me out, and got completely caught up on all my bills.

I loved the job, but then the catch revealed itself. I got served papers for several lawsuits. Then I was advised that there were underground gas tanks that had to be inspected. The tanks were old, and it was likely that they had leaked. I would be responsible for a toxic waste cleanup, and the price tag could go over $1,000,000. Small, independently owned gas stations would completely become a thing of the past. Only big corporations could survive such expensive adjustments.

Gasoline service stations used to have a guy who would pump your gas, clean your windows, check your oil--and he would make a living doing that. When big corporations waste a lot of money-- it means that you have to pump your own gas, and clean your own windows.

You'll get no service, and you'll pay a higher price as ownership is further distanced from you and the people who might be your friends.

My dream had been to own a service station, and at one time owning my own cab. Now I had both, but neither the cab company, nor the gas station were going to last -- they would be devoured by the corporate-government alliance, and I would only be left with liabilities.

Thor was hanging around the cab company all along, and we began arguing about a number of issues. Turmoil at the lot was aggravated because there was confusion amongst the employees about who was boss. I was about to give up my dream, and I felt like a sad song.

Someone walking down the sidewalk had a clarinet. I hollered at them and grabbed it -- then thoroughly irritated Thor by trying to play it. Both of my hands had been crippled -- one because I crushed a Coke bottle on somebody's face, and the other from a gunshot wound, so it was impossible for me to do something like play a clarinet. I found it exciting to try to play it, and especially because it annoyed Thor so much in the midst of one of our final arguments.

Business around town was diminishing as NAFTA made it that the Central Valley was no longer a destination for labor. There were no jobs. Ironic, that the richest agricultural region in the world would be importing food from far away. Something scary was happening, and I wanted to escape.

A couple of the girl's downtown told me that Lady G had gone on a rampage -- kicking in doors on dope dealers, and charging in with an assault rifle. She finally got caught and was in prison. None of the girls ever heard anything about Cat. I never saw Jesus again in Stockton. José had gone to prison. Benjamin Cruz tried to rob the convenience store just down the street from my cab company-- his brother was killed in the attempt, and Ben went to prison.

There were fewer people downtown, and the cops had nothing to do but take away homeless people's shopping carts. At this point, the most interesting person in Stockton was an Egyptian mummy at the Hagan Museum. That mummy could rest to watch over the damned, but I could drive away.

With a clear driving record I could drive taxi in SF.

Caught up on all my bills, I had a car, and I had $600 in my pocket-- it was time to leave.

I drove straight to downtown Oakland – to a pawnshop, and bought a little E flat clarinet. With no idea I'd be able to learn to play -- it didn't matter-- it was somehow symbolic of my escape from Stockton.

I started driving at City Cab in San Francisco.

I had seen the consequence of allowing controls to be distanced from the neighborhood -- and the trickle-down effect of distancing the individual from control over their own lives. Our spirit has traveled too far from home.

A commute of 40 miles is even too much. 10 miles should be the maximum--I could walk that. Yet, I was about to commute to a place 80 miles away. So, I rented my house out to a Hell's Angel, because I figured nobody'd bother the place that way.

I traded my car for a 1950 Ford bus, and parked the bus on the taxi lot in San Francisco. I wasn't planning on going back and forth to Stockton, and the closest I'd come to commuting would be walking the dog. After taking a bite out of hell, I was gone from the misery of Stockton-- back to San Francisco with a cab-driving dog.

To refrain from ill acquaintance, I made friends with a collection of saxophones and clarinets. I'd try to hide in a clarinet for the next few years.

San Francisco would turn out to be less than a blessing...

Before the *Age of Information* many harsh realities were overlooked, but with the new technology that was on the rise even more sordid realities would miss our attention amidst a hurricane of nonsense. Confusion would foster benefits for hierarchy, manipulation, and control. The common man would be reduced to non-beings by numbers in corporate ledgers.

The people of San Francisco were leaving -- displaced by a hoard of zombis. People didn't live in San Francisco anymore... They lived in their phones.

But it doesn't matter *where* you are... What matters is *who* you are. And when every aspect of your life is processed through electronic devices... you will eventually become *nobody*. Such is a more harmful addiction than what I've known.

Relax. Clear your mind. The longer you stop your thoughts the more refined the thoughts that emerge will be.

In our world of rampant informational pollution it may seem more than difficult to break free, but keep trying.

Maintain a simple, objective awareness... the Truth will eventually rise, and magical things may happen.

❖

Confessions from a HELL BOUND TAXI
Book 1: *Introduction to the Real World*
Book 2: *Wicked Women of Misery City*
Book 3: *March of Corporate Technoid Zombis*
Book IV: *The Fences of Freedom*

www.TAXIJAZZ.com

Made in the USA
Columbia, SC
19 April 2025